How To Do Boring, Tedious, Difficult, but *Necessary* Things:
The Art of Sucking It Up and Doing Things You Hate

By Peter Hollins,
Author and Researcher at
petehollins.com

Table of Contents

Introduction 7

Chapter 1: The Cost of a Meaningful Life 11

Chapter 2: How Much Is Enough? 19

Chapter 3: The Meaning of a Slip-Up 27

Chapter 4: Am I improving or am I just afraid to move on? 35

Chapter 5: It's More Important That It's *Done*, Not That You do It 41

Chapter 6: What If You Really Knew You Were Going to Die? 49

Chapter 7: Your Environment Acts on You 55

Chapter 8: Don't Have Yes-Men in Your Life 63

Chapter 9: Improvement Is Not Keeping Up with the Joneses 71

Chapter 10: Put Your Commitments in Black and White 79

Chapter 11: Don't Be Wasteful of Your Time 85

Chapter 12: It's Not Clever, It's Complicated 91

Chapter 13: Don't Forfeit Growth for Comfort 97

Chapter 14: Am I Being Productive or Just Frantic? 105

Chapter 15: Every Yes Is a No, Every No Is a Yes 111

Chapter 16: Master Long-Term Thinking 119

Chapter 17: Understand Controlled, Intentional Risk 127

Chapter 18: Choose Hard Things for an Easier Life 135

Chapter 19: Only Worry About What You Can Control 141

Chapter 20: Apply What You Learn 149

Chapter 21: Don't Speed Read! 155

Chapter 22: The Pygmalion Effect 163

Chapter 23: Stand Firm, No Matter What 169

Chapter 24: The Five-Minute Rule 177

Chapter 25: Understanding Consistency 185

Chapter 26: Make the Right Kind of Mistakes 193

Chapter 27: How Less Can Be More 199

Chapter 28: Learn, But Learn Quickly 207

Chapter 29: Success Is the Sum of Small Efforts 223

Chapter 30: Don't Eliminate Distractions; Eliminate Your Distractibility 229

Conclusion 235

Introduction

Consider Exhibit A: An undisciplined person. This person is impulsive, struggles to follow through on their commitments, and is constantly overwhelmed due to their irregular routine and inability to say no. They fear failure yet paradoxically invite it into their lives with endless procrastination, avoidance, and delay. They feel rushed off their feet and anxious, yet somehow bored and stagnant at the same time. Their poor lifestyle habits and addiction to instant gratification means their finances, relationships, and personal growth are all sabotaged.

Now, compare this picture with Exhibit B: A disciplined person. This person has ups and downs, but they have a sense of stability, consistency, and resilience from their routines and good habits, and this creates a lasting feeling of self-control and inner regulation. This person sets goals and takes action. They achieve. They develop over time. They are purpose-driven, organized, and responsible – *constantly*. They experience bad days and temptation, but this doesn't seem to matter one bit when it comes to their commitment.

The fact that there are disciplined and undisciplined people in the world won't be news to anyone. The big question is *why*. What exactly makes one person self-controlled and focused, while another cannot seem to gather themselves towards a clearly identified goal?

Is it intelligence? No – many undisciplined people are exceptionally bright.

Is it aptitude? No – many undisciplined people are very talented and capable.

Is it a lack of knowledge or education? Again, no – undisciplined people know exactly what they should do and why. They just don't do it.

The truth is that discipline is not a question of intelligence, capability, or knowledge. It's not a question of motivation or courage or willpower. Disciplined people are the way they are, and do the things they do, because of their *perspective*.

Disciplined people think in a distinctive way about themselves and about life. The mental frame they place around their actions and choices is precisely what enables them to build a life of order, purpose, growth, and clarity.

In this book, we will explore not just the habits and methods favored by disciplined people, but the underlying mindset that gives rise to them. What follows are thirty essays, one for each day of the month. Think of them as a series of snapshots taken of the mind of a disciplined person. Our goal is not mere mimicry, but to carefully absorb and internalize these attitudes until they become our own.

The way we think influences the way we feel.

The way we feel influences the way we act.

The way we act influences the people we become.

In that case, becoming a disciplined person starts in the mind.

Chapter 1: The Cost of a Meaningful Life

Most of us at some point in our lives have said, "I need to be a bit more disciplined," or "I'm quitting today – I mean it, I'm done."

Saying you want a better life is one thing. But we won't begin our book with a consideration of all the great things a person might desire of life – health, wellbeing, creativity, self-control, fulfilment, success, and so on.

Instead of asking, "What do I want in life?" we're going to ask a more honest, more useful question: "What's your budget?"

By this I mean, how much is it worth to you? How much are you willing to pay? In other words, what are you actually bringing to the table to put towards that thing you say you want?

It might be the easiest thing in the world to identify a sincere desire to achieve a yearned-for goal, whether that's starting a new business venture, writing a novel, learning an instrument, mastering a new language, acquiring a valuable skill, or overcoming personal limitations to reach your fullest potential.

What is more difficult is being honest about how much that costs, so to speak. The bill is always a little eye-watering: the business venture takes immense courage and hard work; the novel takes patience and stamina; the instrument demands an almost supernatural ability to tolerate boredom and slow, slow, slow progress; the language takes a willingness to make mistakes... lots of them.

What if I told you that all it would take to be a more disciplined, effective, and fulfilled human being is to invest one solid, quality hour of your time each and every day to the endeavor, from now until the day you die?

Perhaps you'd think, "A whole hour? Wait, every single day forever... even on weekends?"

Or perhaps you'd think, "Only one hour? That's all? That's nothing, if it would make me a more disciplined, effective, and fulfilled human being. What a bargain."

The Five-Hour Rule

One of the biggest mindset shifts that accompanies a genuine transformation into more discipline and self-determination is to realize that being a more disciplined person is not something you *have to* do – it's something you *get* to do. It's an opt-in experience.

The five-hour rule is a way of training yourself to make better choices every day, as a matter of habit. The five-hour rule requires you to practice consistency, delayed gratification, and focus in the face of distraction.

The idea is simple: You invest one quality hour of your time per day, five times a week, towards those activities that yield long-term growth. You defend this little hour against fleeting distractions, complaints, and shapeless, undisciplined mediocrity. This daily hour is for the good stuff – improvement, growth, genuine productivity, reflection. It's not for mindless entertainment or distraction.

The value is certainly in the hour itself, and what you "spend" it on, but it's also in all those aspects of your character you will need to strengthen to effectively honor this daily appointment with yourself, no matter what. There is additional value in merely continuing to show up when you say you will.

You may have a daily temptation to skip or "forget" your hour, but with the five-hour rule, you are blessed to have a daily opportunity to teach you the lesson of sticking to it anyway. You learn to resist impulsivity and to stay connected and committed to your goals even though the easiest thing in the world would be to let them quietly slip from your hands.

Over time, you teach yourself that when it comes to achieving the things that really matter to you in life, an hour a day really is nothing. Nearly everyone would like to be more disciplined. Let's imagine that the bare minimum entrance fee to ride that ride is a mere hour a day. Instead of asking about the things I need to do to be more disciplined, it may be wiser to first ask – *Am I actually prepared to invest the time required to do all those things?*

The Three Buckets

OK, so let's say the five-hour budget is doable for you.

Now, what will you do with that hour?

We can break the range of possible activities into three main buckets: *reading*, *reflecting*, and *experimenting*. Here's how you can do it:

Train Your FOCUS Through Reading

Tomas Corley, author of *Rich Habits: The Daily Success Habits of Wealthy Individuals*, found that two thirds of the people he classified as wealthy did not watch TV, and an impressive 86% of them read books with the express intention of learning and development.

Chance Maddox muses that the average millionaire comfortably reads two or more books a month; and that's not all, successful people cram every spare moment they have with learning: They listen to audiobooks on their commute, they browse long-form news and blog articles while waiting at the doctor's office, and they listen to podcasts while tidying up after dinner.

The content matters, of course, but if you're interested in cultivating more self-discipline, the magic is really in the consistent, repeated choice to focus the energy you have on what is enriching instead of worthless entertainment, or the distractions and inanities that culture tries to pass off as "relaxation."

If an hour a day feels a little intimidating, don't worry. Even the weakest reading muscles can strengthen if you start small and challenge yourself to do just five minutes more than the time before. Choose that focus.

Strengthen Mental CLARITY Through Reflection

Discipline isn't just about maximizing the doing, but about clarifying the *direction* of the doing – what is the point of all this effort in the first place? What does it lead to? Focus, efficiency, and power mean nothing unless they're in service of some genuinely meaningful goal – a goal outlined in your mind's eye with crisp, detailed precision.

Stop.

What are you doing?

Why are you doing it?

Reflecting in this way helps you cut a meaningful path through the noise and irrelevances. Reflection helps you clearly and quickly identify when you are lost and need to correct course.

What are your values? What are your long-, medium- and short-term goals? How well are you achieving those goals? What can you do more of... and less of?

Without reflection, it's easy for your efforts to be co-opted towards the service of someone else's goals and values. Instead, use your daily hour to stay intentional and self-aware of exactly where you are willing to spend yourself, and why.

Build GRIT Through Experimentation

Real discipline isn't about playing it safe. There isn't much value in being an automaton who has perfect discipline but only uses it to execute the same set of choreographed maneuvers over and over again.

Discipline is also about opening an arena for experimentation. Try, fail, and adjust. In other words, learning and evolution are the result of a consistent willingness to engage in trial-and-error.

Your daily hour is not just for empty abstraction, but for putting theories into action. Devise tests, send feelers out into the unknown, take risks, and practice a posture of curiosity rather than complacency. The more you train yourself to take risks and adapt in small ways every day, the less you'll hesitate when it really matters.

The Bottom Line:

We all want the good things in life. But how much are we willing to pay for them?

For five short hours a week, you can make gains in focus, clarity, and grit.

Distractions and temptations are constant. They crop up and make us an offer that feels hard to refuse: "Wouldn't you rather just have this fun, easy thing over here, this thing that doesn't cost you anything, and you can have it right now?"

Being disciplined means being willing to answer that temptation with firm resolution: "No. The thing I want is valuable. It is **worth** the effort and hard work. I am willing to pay that. I **choose** to pay that."

It's not about how bad you want something, it's about what you're willing to pay to get it.

Chapter 2: How Much Is Enough?

For many of us, the battle for self-discipline plays out in the fact that we live in a world of infinitely renewing temptations, presented on a never-ending carousel. A glut of things to quench any desire, supplied constantly.

There is *more than enough* food.

There is *more than enough* entertainment.

There is *more than enough* comfort, ease, relaxation, and even luxury.

And yet, we struggle to find the limit, say no, and establish some sense of contentment and sufficiency when all that's available is excess.

To our distant ancestors, the world did not possess this kind of sickening overabundance, and the phrase "more than enough" must have seemed like a good thing. Modern man, though, suffers under this oversaturation. The story of addiction, burnt out, and overstimulated boredom tells us that "more than enough" may also be read as "too much."

When is enough enough?

Modern man answers, "When it's enough, plus a little extra, just in case."

One possible alternative: "When it's just a little less than enough, just in case."

Hara Hachi Bu

Hara Hachi Bu (腹八分目) is a Japanese eating practice that translates to "Eat until you're 80% full." The idea is said to have originated in Okinawa and is an eating habit associated with a broader philosophy of sufficiency and minimalism.

This eating habit is associated with better digestion, lower rates of disease, and a longer life expectancy. Unsurprisingly, Okinawans have relatively low BMIs. Instead of eating *beyond* the point of satisfaction, the idea is to just barely attain satiation or preferably leave yourself in a slight deficit.

Satiety, scientists tell us, is a physiological sensation of fullness in the body; it's the state of hunger being satisfied and is mediated by certain chemical signals in the body. It takes around 5-20 minutes minutes to manifest in the conscious mind. Practically speaking, only eating up to 80% fullness gives your body time to catch up, preventing you from accidentally overeating in that short window.

But satiety is not just a physiological state. *It's a psychological condition of gratitude, sufficiency, satisfaction, and contentment.* It is the opposite of want and desire. Enough, they say, is as good as a feast. Restrained contentment, then, is just as good as the fulfilment of an infinite number of your wildest dreams.

Hara Hachi Bu is a deliberate exercise in self-discipline. It requires control, mindfulness, and the ability to make intentional choices rather than acting on impulse. It also requires we do something that feels wildly frightening and counterintuitive: willfully choosing to go without.

It is possible to teach yourself that observing limits does not diminish you, but in fact strengthens and calms you. Rather than reactively answering the beck and call of every petty desire that arises in us, we train ourselves to leave space. To choose to have what we already have. To experience the beauty and luxury and perfection of *enough*.

Do we need more than we have?

Do we even need everything that we have?

When we eat 120% of what we need, we somehow still want more. When we eat 80% of what we need, we realize it is, in some strange way, enough.

Applying the Hara Hachi Bu Mindset to Other Areas of Life

The principle of Hara Hachi Bu can help ease addiction and overconsumption of all kinds, replacing it with a gentler, more moderate attitude. If you're pouring yourself a glass of water, would you keep pouring and pouring, even beyond the point where the water reached the rim and flowed over? Would you keep pouring so that water spilled all over the kitchen counter and onto the floor?

When it comes to consumption and training yourself to recognize enough, self-discipline is simply having the wisdom to realize that excess is not an improvement on sufficiency. Epictetus said, "Nothing is enough for the man to whom enough is too little."

A disciplined mind understands the peace that comes from having limits, both *internal* and *external*. It understands that you don't always need to get everything you want, nor do you always need to give everything you have.

Know When to Log Off

Push yourself. Give 110%. Break through your limits.

Or should you?

Perhaps overworking is a sign not of your valiant self-discipline, but of your inability to identify that point where you can confidently say, "I've done enough."

But working hard, striving for your dreams, and being dedicated are all good things. Can you really have "too much of a good thing?" This is a question we should ask someone who has recently eaten five slices of cake.

Just as Hara Hachi Bu teaches you to stop eating before you're uncomfortably full, stopping work before the point of exhaustion leads to a more harmonious, balanced, and sustainable work ethic over time.

Pushing past the point of focus only leads to diminishing returns, anyway. It's as though you are pouring and pouring, but all that extra water is just going to waste, and in fact giving you something you now have to clean up.

Sometimes, it feels like discipline means treating yourself like a drill segreant and not taking no for an answer.

But sometimes, discipline means having the courage to say, "*This* is what my best looks like right now, and that is enough." Another opportunity to work will come. We all have limits, and there is no prize at the end of life for forcing your way through yours. Pace yourself. Take time to digest.

Give in Relationships, But Don't Overextend

The nature of human desire is that it's theoretically unlimited. Consciously honoring limits is a choice we make – it will seldom be made by someone else on our behalf.

The same things can be said of the nature of human compassion, generosity, and the desire to do good. While there may be something romantic in the notion of unlimited generosity and absolute kindness, the fact is that the limits to our ability to give are about as fixed as the limits of our stomach to receive.

Applying Hara Hachi Bu to relationships means being present, kind, and giving, while also respecting your own limits so that you aren't totally depleted. Boundaries can be thought of as fences placed around valuable resources to protect and preserve them. Farmers keep back a little seed from every harvest to secure next year's crop; in the same way, commit yourself, but always keep a little back so that you can replenish again.

Progress Without Obsession

Ambition, determination, and drive are valuable. But then there is obsessively chasing the next milestone, propelled by a deeper undercurrent of anxiety: the worry that you do not have enough, that there is not enough, and that you are not enough.

Self-improvement is most lasting and genuine when it comes from a place of sincere desire for growth, expansion, and development. When it comes from a panicked desire to "fix" a perceived lack, it quickly becomes a hole that can never be filled. Focus on one milestone, do it fully and well, then move onto the next. Pause to celebrate and incorporate new accomplishments, rather than hurrying immediately on to the next box to tick.

The Bottom Line:

Good things do not have to be infinite to be good or to have value.

This includes the things we consume, but also the things we produce – the work we do, the time we give, and the demands we place on ourselves and our capacity.

Enough is enough.

Chapter 3: The Meaning of a Slip-Up

Let's imagine you made a promise to yourself to stay off a particular social media site for a month. You know it fries your nervous system, shatters your attention span, dulls your humanity, and fritters away your precious waking hours on brain rot that brings nothing of value to your life. You know all of that.

But on Day 4 you cave and find yourself right back at that poisoned watering hole again. It's twenty minutes before you can tear yourself away again and face the sinking sensation of having failed. The question is, now what?

Many of us fail to be disciplined because we don't plan properly. We plan for that best-case scenario, but we don't walk ourselves through all the other possibilities. So now one mistake means that the entire plan is void. That pristine "30 Days" concept is now broken, after all, and all you have is your measly 3-day run.

What does a mistake or slip-up like this *mean*?

The way you answer that question will determine what you do next.

It's common to see a slip-up as a totalizing force; it's something that by its mere existence cancels out all the grandest and sincerity of the resolution we held onto up to that point. It's like a dead mouse in a water tank – there's no way around it; the entire water tank is discarded.

It's more productive (and less stressful), however, to *minimize* a slip-up, instead of playing it up in this way. When you see mistakes and slip-ups as normal, predictable, and very much part of the plan, then you don't have to throw the entire plan away. You can continue on with it as soon as you're aware of the mistake and willing to let it go.

If you make a mistake mean a lot, then it means a lot – it's elevated to the role of a catastrophe that can and must be allowed to derail you.

But if you make a mistake mean only as much as it means – and no more – then you can carry on with the plan as soon as possible.

Imagine that an artist, for reasons known only to himself, wants to drop 1000 dots of white paint onto a large black canvas, all in a perfect, neat grid. This task requires a steady hand and a consistent technique to make all 1000 dots as similar as possible. It requires absolute focus, and a still mind.

Naturally, he makes a mistake. When he paints dot number 14, the artist's attention wanders, and the paint dot smudges. He looks at the dot and is filled with despair and disappointment. Now what?

This dot is certainly a failure. But is the whole painting a failure? Well, the painting hasn't been completed yet. If the artist did complete it, and worked hard to not let his attention wander again, and produced all the other dots perfectly, would this lone bad dot spoil the picture? Probably not.

Even if several of the dots were bad, it wouldn't matter. There would be *so many* good dots that the bad dots would visually disappear. We can think of our own mistakes, failures and slip ups in the same way. The only way they can be "diluted" is by adding more and more occasions when we *do* step up and do what we intended to do.

The trick is not to throw the painting in the trash and start over. The trick is not to give up. The trick is simply to keep adding as many good dots as possible. Especially when starting out, a mistake can feel like an end. If it's your very first dot, you indeed have a 100% failure rate. But by simply adding just one more good dot, your failure rate is halved.

No matter how bad the mistake is that you made, your next best move is *always* to try again and make the right choice.

The Two-Day Rule

The two-day rule is simple, but powerful: **Commit to *never* skipping a productive habit for more than two days in a row.**

There are a million reasons why you might slip up, forget, or have a genuine excuse for not being able to follow through consistently on a good habit. One day is understandable. One day is forgivable. One day is comfortably within the margin of normal human fallibility. Perfection is not possible.

But you do not have to let one day become two days. Whenever you slip up, you are like the painter staring at that malformed dot number 14. At that moment, you have a choice. You can allow your next move to be defined by this mistake, or you can discount the mistake, and let your continued commitment and intention decide your next move.

It may feel hard to get back on track if you're disappointed, guilty, angry, embarrassed, or defeated. Luckily, immediately taking inspired action in the right direction is arguably the single most effective way of overcoming these negative feelings. Dwelling on them, however, means you risk allowing that mistake to mean more than it has to.

Remind yourself that a single mistake is not yet a failure, and you have not yet spiraled back down to your old habits. You are only officially on that spiral when you follow up that mistake with another one just like it.

The two-day rule works because it makes room for imperfection, while keeping you on the path of consistency. Repetition strengthens your neural pathways, and what you repeat over time only becomes easier to repeat. A one-day lapse can be easily accommodated by a broadly intact habit; but a two-day lapse starts gaining its own momentum and is harder to recover from.

Respond Before the Clock Runs Out

Procrastination is like putting down a no-dot on the canvas. It's a delay and a missed opportunity. However, when you think about it, a stubborn bout of procrastination always begins with choosing to delay what is objectively a small task – and doing just the first step is often a lot less work than it seems.

It's OK to say "I'll just do it later" now and then. But the longer you let something sit, the more likely it is to keep on sitting. The irony is that with procrastination, the angst and guilt and worry about not acting is often far more unpleasant than the slight discomfort of just taking that first step. If an email requires a thoughtful response, don't ignore it past the next day—at the very least, acknowledge receipt or set a reminder.

Don't Go More Than Two Days Without a "Glimmer"

Self-discipline isn't just about work. Sometimes, we need to deliberately train our attention onto all the good things in life we'd ordinarily take for granted. Maintain balance by making sure that you never go two days in a row where you don't stop to appreciate a "glimmer."

This is a little moment of peace, joy, or gratitude in life, a little flutter of poignancy that gives life its color and dimension. When adversity inevitably comes, it will land into a life peppered with little moments of brightness and meaning. Resilience means feeling as though difficulties are temporary, while what is permanent is your continued willingness to bounce back to a baseline of gratitude and wellbeing.

Reset Quickly After a Setback

The two-day rule is effective because it balances self-compassion with accountability. You're allowed to slip, but it's also your job to get back on track. Though it seems like a paradox, forgiveness and high standards can live in the same universe. There is a higher-order self-discipline which understands that ultimately, we are the ones who take responsibility for ourselves. We need to be able to be kind enough to ourselves to forgive mistakes, tough enough on ourselves to do the right thing, and honest enough to know precisely where the line is between them.

The Bottom Line:

What does a mistake mean? It doesn't have to mean *anything*, if you follow it up as quickly as possible with conscious, intentional action.

Once is a mistake. Twice is a pattern. Three times is a habit.

Chapter 4: Am I improving or am I just afraid to move on?

When people are asked about their flaws and they say, "perfectionism," it feels like a cop-out. It's a little like saying ,"I'm the humblest person you'll ever meet," or "I'm pretty, but I don't know it." It's tempting to think of perfectionism as a flaw but a highly noble and virtuous one, like loving your wife too much.

But what if perfectionism actually *is* a weakness?

Perfectionism is a little like that skill of being able to throw your voice so that it seems like it's coming from the other end of the room. We may distract others and even ourselves with images of the ideal, of our own high standards, and our painstaking attention to detail, all the while our attention is drawn away from what's in the other corner: an inability to tolerate evaluation, risk avoidance, and a desire to be in control.

Progress is a series of steps of incremental improvements. Unless you are willing to accept that some of those steps are not perfect, and to move on from those imperfections, then progress is a logical impossibility. If you are terrified of failure, of being judged or criticized, or if you're trapped in an endless loop of insignificant revisions and adjustments, then you will either never begin, or you'll never really stop, ultimately delaying results that could already be making an impact. Either way, real progress and improvement are forfeited.

The perfectionist mind says, "It's all-or-nothing." Either it's perfect, or it's garbage. The sad thing is that you more often end up with the "nothing" than the "all."

Perfection, if it exists, is something that emerges over time, as a result of compounding actions. A complete project moves you forward, and it moves you forward even if it does contain a few imperfections. An unfinished project does precisely nothing to move you forward, no matter how perfect it *could* be.

Choose Done Over Perfect

"Perfection" is lovely, but it's not real. It's always a future promise, an ideal, a hope. It's not bankable. "Complete," on the other hand, has one characteristic that beats anything perfection has: it actually exists in the world.

On the surface, perfectionism may seem like a dedication to quality, but it often results in missed deadlines and wasted time. Knowing how to tolerate "good enough" and move on requires a special kind of discipline.

Identify When "Refining" Becomes "Stalling"

"Tweaks" can be a trap. Wasting time endlessly refining minor details can temporarily alleviate anxiety because it genuinely does feel like you're doing something. But are you making substantial changes that are going to meaningfully improve the overall task?

Adjustments and corrections *do* improve a work, to a certain extent. However, if you find yourself endlessly revising and re-revising the same things, it may be time to ask if there's something you're avoiding. Perfectionism is a complicated plant with long roots that sometimes come from unexpected places. Completing a project can be scary because it might lead to judgment, criticism, or to something potentially worse

– praise and the dialing up of demands and expectations.

Set Time Limits

If you make "perfection" your yardstick, you burden yourself with the mission of achieving the unachievable and finishing the unfinishable. You assign yourself a task that can be done a million different ways except perfectly, and then also assert, "I will accept none of these… I will only accept perfection."

This is self-sabotage.

Perfectionism blooms in the absence of clear boundaries. Instead of making a lofty, abstract ideal your goal, challenge yourself to set smaller, more concrete goals down here on earth. Set strict time limits – when the time is up, it's up, and there's no arguing with it, no room for "just one more tweak." Time stops you from over-investing in projects that are already as good as they need to be and prevents you neglecting other tasks that actually require your attention. Set the timer, do your best, and when the time is up, move on.

Accept That Good Enough is Often Better Than Perfect

The fear of other people's judgment is often not grounded in reality. Some parents are overly critical and demanding in their expectations. They can instill in their children the faulty belief that the world out there is ready to pounce on the smallest and most insignificant flaws of their every effort. In reality, most people are not that cruel, nor are they that attentive. If people expect something of you, they almost always prefer to just have that thing, minor imperfections included, instead of having to wait while you make endless adjustments that they don't require.

When it comes to delivering finished work, hesitation and delay can convey unreliability and a lack of confidence. A great project submitted precisely on time has more value than a perfect project delivered two days too late.

There is a darker side to perfectionism, and you can use your own discretion to decide whether it applies to you or not. While perfectionism may stem from rejection sensitivity, feelings of inadequacy, or even OCD, it can just as much be fueled by vanity, rivalry, an unreasonable desire for praise and recognition, or the need to be perceived as masterful and competent. The overlap between perfectionism and narcissism has been a point of interest for researchers for some time (Smith et. al., 2016, *Perfectionism and narcissism: A meta-analytic review*). If this is ringing a bell, an illuminating question may be, who am I to expect perfection?

The Bottom Line:

Perfectionism is self-sabotaging behavior masquerading as a commitment to quality and high standards. By setting a hard time limit, doing your best, and moving swiftly on, you allow for genuine progress.

Done is better than perfect.

Chapter 5: It's More Important That It's *Done*, Not That You do It

There is a mythology of heroism surrounding any exploit of self-discipline or personal development. The business world tells us that successful, strong individuals are just that – individuals. Winners are stubbornly self-sufficient, with bootstraps of iron. They battle personal demons, they dig deep into private reserves, and their resulting triumphs are theirs and theirs alone.

This illusion may be an inspiring one, but it is still just an illusion. A genuinely helpful skill to learn is that of delegation — learning to consciously and willingly hand over authority, control, and trust to someone else. It's the discipline to prioritize the completion of a task over any desire or expectation that *we* should be the ones to do it.

There are plenty of reasons to prefer that we and we alone are in charge. Most of them bogus.

Lack of Trust in Others

When something feels important to us, it can be difficult to let others in on it. We may not have much faith in their ability to really *get* it like we do.

Lack of Willingness to Value Others' Contributions

Perfectionism is sometimes the most exhausting vanity to maintain. The ego may simply not be willing to acknowledge the value others can bring to a project – a value that may not only complement and bolster our own contributions, but even exceed them.

Fear of Losing Control

It's anxiety-provoking to be at the mercy of other people's actions, and it may feel easier to just shoulder certain responsibilities yourself.

Lack of Clarity

Delegating can feel hard simply because when we have a lack of clarity on the importance of different aspects of a job, we default to the assumption that *everything* is vital and therefore everything must be our job.

These are the things that get in the way of successfully delegating, managing yourself and others, and collaborating effectively. *Should* you delegate and let others be involved? The answer to that question is the same as the one you give to this question: "What's more important, that this is done, or that this is done by me specifically?"

Delegate Effectively with the PAT Framework

If you have the discipline to accept "done" instead of "done by me," then there are some practical ways to address the various impediments to effective delegation.

Trying to handle everything yourself is not heroic, it's egoic. It drains your energy and resources and narrows your perspective. No matter how hardworking you are, you do not have infinite time on your hands. Delegating isn't about avoiding responsibility — it's about strategically directing your focus where it truly matters while allowing others to take care of tasks that don't require your direct involvement.

The Stoic philosophers understood that a well-lived life was not about successfully bringing as much of your circumstances under your control as possible. Rather, wisdom for the Stoics meant learning to discern between what is rightfully under your control, and what is simply not in your domain.

We cannot control how other people perform, what they understand, and exactly how they will manage a task we assign to them. What we can control, however, is our own Stoic sense of discernment. We can take responsibility for learning to delegate as effectively as possible.

If you don't know where to start with delegation, Colin Boyd's PAT framework is a simple and effective starting point. Common fears around delegating tasks boil down to the simple worry that others just won't do the task properly. One way to mitigate this fear is to clearly communicate expectations up front, rather than anxiously micromanaging the details once the task is already out of your hands. Good delegation, then, is just as much about clear and precise instructions as it is about lowering our anxiety about having those instructions properly followed.

Purpose — Explain Why It Matters

We feel possessive over a task not because of the task, but because of what that task *means* to us, and what it represents in our world. To encourage other people to take ownership of a task, it's not enough to simply outline a task; the purpose behind that task needs to be known.

When you are handing over a task, also hand over the bigger picture in which that task belongs. This means that you are valuing the task, but also implicitly valuing that person's responsibility and role in bringing that task about.

You already may see the value in doing the task well, but delegating properly means that you can explain to others why they too should want to do it well. Nobody wants to spend time or effort on pointless activities; people are more willing to invest in those tasks where they can see a direct link between their effort and some greater purpose. Explain what needs to be done, and *why*.

Action — Outline What Needs to Be Done Clearly

A big reason tasks don't turn out as we expect is simply a lack of clear instructions. Instead of assuming someone knows what you want, break the task into steps. Be as specific as necessary while leaving room for autonomy. If you're worried about mistakes, ask them to check in after the first step so you can course-correct early.

Timeframe — Set a Deadline Without Hovering

A common fear is losing control of timing. Set a clear and unambiguous deadline upfront, and be sure to mutually agree on a time, potentially framing the request as a question. Asking for explicit agreement on a deadline doesn't just confirm the other person's ability to deliver on time, but it also activates their sense of personal accountability. If a person is working hard to meet a deadline they feel they have in essence set for themselves, then there is no need, for you or for them, to hover around and micromanage with prompts, check-ins, or reminders.

Example:

> "I need you to compile some well-organized client data that we'll need to help us make an important decision

in the budget meeting on Friday afternoon (**P**urpose). Here's what I need: First, label the files by client name, then draw up a summary sheet, and lastly, upload everything to the shared drive (**A**ction). Can you have this done by Friday morning latest, let's say 11 a.m.? (**T**imeframe). Please ask me if you have any questions, but let's touch base Wednesday morning so I can make sure everything's on track."

The Bottom Line:

No matter how hardworking, passionate, or invested we are, we are limited in the time, resources, and skill we can devote to any one project. It takes discipline to apply yourself to your work to the fullest of your potential; it also takes discipline to recognize those tasks that simply do not require your direct personal involvement.

Let go of low-priority work and let go of work that others can do better or more quickly than you can. This frees you up to apply greater discipline where it matters.

Pick good people to do the work you need them to and have the discipline not to interfere with them while they do it.

Chapter 6: What If You Really Knew You Were Going to Die?

Of course you know you're going to die.

But what if you *really* knew it?

What if this concept wasn't just an abstract concept to you, but something you keenly felt, something at the front and center of your mind, something that could not help but influence all your thoughts, feelings, and decisions?

For most of us, death is not really real. It's something that happens to other people, in other places, at other times. We "know" what death is in the same way that we know about the existence of atoms or other countries – it's something we haven't truly seen or touched; it's a placc we have never been.

Memento Mori

Memento mori is Latin for Remember that you will die.

A man may experience a frightening brush with death and have an unexpected and embarrassing encounter with his own mortality. He is terrified. In the wake of his mortality, however, he is stunned to realize that the frightening thing is not the yawning black abyss of the unknown; rather, it's the worthless life lived *before* that day; the life that could have been lived, but wasn't. "It is not death that man should fear," Marcus Aurelius said, "but he should fear never beginning to live."

They say that hell is truth seen too late. Memento mori should make us afraid, but of what? Not the fear of obliteration, but the fear that there should be nothing to obliterate. In his novel *All the Light We Cannot See*, Anthony Doerr writes, "Open your eyes and see what you can with them before they close forever."

What if you lived your life, right now, today, as if you really believed that you were not in fact immortal, and that your days were numbered? What if you never let yourself forget that your life – everything you know and feel yourself to be – is not permanent, and that literally everything you have today may be forever taken away from you tomorrow?

The idea is not to immobilize yourself with despair, but to spur a healthy sense of urgency. We can choose to live our life in countless different ways, but when the final door at the end of being closes for us, it doesn't open again, and we will not be invited to redo any of it.

What, then, is our intention?

What is our light and existence *for*, if it must be hemmed in on either side by darkness and non-existence?

At its core, memento mori anchors us in the reality that our time here on this earth is finite. The implications of this fact, if fully grasped, lead to a mindset that naturally supports self-discipline. When one sees that every day — and every decision — *counts*, procrastination begins to feel less like a harmless delay and more like a forfeited opportunity.

When these moments we have are limited, we can appreciate the necessity of making them matter. Memento mori teaches us gratitude. A common hypothetical is to ask, "What would you today if you were going to die tomorrow?"

However, there is no "if" in this question. The exact details of how and when are unknown, but we *will* die tomorrow, in a manner of speaking. And it is not a hypothetical. We really do need to ask ourselves with utmost gravity, "What will I do today?"

When we say, "I'll do it tomorrow," we are making the gravest error. Tomorrow has not been given. Are we entitled to start making plans for something that was never guaranteed to us? All we are given is today, or more accurately, we are only given a single slender moment that stands before us, the present.

Instead of taking this moment, the most precious thing we have and could hope to have, and treating it like it has no value, we could be like those ancient Stoics and make a discipline of remembering – remembering that none of this lasts forever. The classic memento mori is to display a human skull where you, busy in your endless distractions and irrelevances, can see it every day. You remember that it is only time that separates your own skull from the fate of this one. You realize with relief that, for now at least, it pleases the gods that you live. In humble gratitude, you set aside laziness and fear, and get to work.

Less gothic forms of memento mori are available for modern man:

Your days are numbered. This is a fact that may be a little easier to absorb visually. Create a chart with 80 rows (representing 80 years of life) and 52 columns (for 52 weeks per year). Each cell represents one week of your precious, finite life. Blot out all the weeks already lived. Those are done, forever. They are irreplaceable. Then, turn your attention to the remaining cells – bright little squares of living possibility.

At the end of every week, take that bright open square and color it in, and commit it to the grave. Did it live a good life?

If this approach seems a little morbid, remind yourself that time really is passing in this way, whether you track it or not. In fact, 80 years is an optimistic estimate, and many of us may find that our given portion of life falls short of this.

Use the discomfort you feel to inspire more consistency, more self-discipline, and more focused and intentional living for the time you have left. Because while life is indeed falling away from us one little block at a time, it's also true that as long as we live, we have an astoundingly valuable gift: the opportunity to take this day, this moment, and make it mean something.

The Bottom Line:

How would you live if you really knew you were going to die?

Be present and live with all of yourself, right now, while you have the chance. Do not fritter away your life and time with the expectation that you can somehow make it up later.

Don't wait and delay. Be a good person, now.

The greatest tragedy is not death, but life lived without purpose.

Chapter 7: Your Environment Acts on You

If you walk into a plush, cozy living room that is well-furnished with sofas and comfortable rugs and throws, what do you do? You probably relax. You sit down, maybe take a nap.

What do you do when you walk into a dark, smoky bar where the only seat is at a table with some rowdy drunk philosophers who are caught up in a raucous debate? You sit down, order a drink, and maybe weigh in, quickly getting embroiled in the argument.

If you walk into a pristine, ordered library, with a gramophone in one corner quietly playing Chopin, and a kind old man painting watercolors in the other, what do you do? Perhaps you idly take a book off the shelves and start to read. Maybe you sit quietly for a while, listening to the music, or just watching as the old man daubs colors onto the paper...

The boundary around a person's will is porous. It can be acted upon.

An environment is not some neutral backdrop, but a constant and active influence on us. An environment is itself a set of values, because it allows for only a limited number of possible actions, while cutting off the possibility of all other actions. In the same way that a comfy sofa invites a very particular action from us (relaxing, napping) the broader environment of our life itself exerts a constant and active influence over the actions that feel most likely and possible at any one point in time.

Surrounding Yourself with the Right People

It is as difficult to be disciplined in an undisciplined environment as it is to be alert and productive in a soft, cozy living room. In life, the greatest influence on how we act is often not our own free will or conscious choice, but rather the collective impact of the various people surrounding us.

If you are in the company of a complaining, irritable person, the most likely action for *you* to take is to passively join in on the grumbling. Likewise, if all your friends are new parents, horse-riding fanatics, or gamers, you may find that a significant portion of all conversations you have will heavily feature children, horses, or games.

While we cannot help but be influenced by the people that make up our world, we do have some say over who we allow into that world. We can look at the environments in which our life plays out and ask whether their influence on us is making self-discipline more or less likely.

There are some people who will make it feel like it's almost impossible to do the self-disciplined thing. On the other hand, there are people who have the opposite effect – their mere presence can make it seem like the only possible course of action is to be self-disciplined. Who are those people?

Cut Out the Negative Influences

There are certain friendships and social dynamics built on an unspoken mutual agreement to quietly let one another off the hook. "I'll agree to give you permission to be lazy, if you agree to give me the same permission." While good friendships naturally have a degree of comfort and non-judgment, the truth is that surrounding yourself with people who make a habit of inaction will only lead to your own stagnation.

People may have all sorts of reasons why they can't or won't. Try to distance yourself from such influences so you don't adopt these excuses as your own over time. Instead, seek out people who not only believe in the possibility of growth and progress, but those who believe in *your* potential specifically.

Be cautious about those whose acceptance and kindness are conditional on you playing small, as they may unconsciously sabotage any effort you make to improve. Pay attention to how people respond to your enthusiasm to be more disciplined. If they match it and ask what they can do to support you, that's a good sign.

Seek Out Smarter, More Disciplined Peers

It's comfortable to be surrounded by people who are like you and agree with you. It's pleasant to be the smartest or most accomplished person in the room. However, if real growth is your goal, then you need to surround yourself with people who will press and challenge you to do more, rather than those who praise and affirm what you've already done. Associate with people who are dedicated, disciplined, committed, skilled, experienced, motivated, and resilient. Remember that you are porous, and their energy will rub off on you.

Not every friend needs to be a mentor or a teacher. But we do need mentors and teachers. One of the greatest skills you may ever acquire is the ability to identify and connect with those people who are comfortably operating merely one level up from you. You don't need an all-knowing guru or master — just strive to learn from a person who has recently overcome the challenges that preoccupy you currently.

Let their achievements inspire you to raise your baseline. Learn from their example. Be curious about their mistakes and take steps to avoid them on your own journey. This will keep you humble and honest, driven by the aspiration for something better up ahead.

Stay Close to Excellence, Even Virtually

It's not necessarily the case that the most accomplished among us are the most excellent. What matters is not ability or achievement, but mindset. We may learn more about the art of excellent discipline from a beginner than from a complacent expert who has long fallen out of the habit.

Bearing in mind that self-discipline is a virtue that runs through all excellent endeavors, we do not need to limit ourselves to mentors and role models who are working in the same line of work that we are. We can learn patience, diligence, consistency, humility, etc., from someone even if we have nothing in common with them other than a desire to do the thing we are doing *well*.

If it's difficult for you to access quality role models in person, then access them some other way; what matters is that you are being exposed to their ideas and mindset. Read their books, listen to their podcasts, join online communities, or attend talks and workshops. Learn from a distance. By furnishing your own internal environment with ideas of excellence, virtue, and self-determination, it becomes habitual for you. Soon, consistent, disciplined habit will feel like the only viable choice you can make.

The Bottom Line:

Does my environment encourage or hinder my self-discipline?

Your mindset is influenced by your environment, and the people you interact with most often. Choose to be in environments and around people who make unfolding of the best version of yourself possible.

Unfold your life in the presence of the inspired, the disciplined, the honest, and the grateful.

Chapter 8: Don't Have Yes-Men in Your Life

Surround yourself with positive people.

Surround yourself with people who make you happy, people you can laugh with, people who will accept you for who you are.

Surround yourself with people who will support you and believe in your greatness.

This is common advice. But is it good advice?

Sometimes, the most positive thing we can learn is to be negative — to say no, whether to ourselves or to others.

Sometimes, our "happiness" can be deadly, if it means that we prioritize ease, comfort, and self-satisfaction over being realistic, humble, or diligent.

Sometimes, what we need is not flattery, but honesty. We need someone to hold us accountable, not someone to indulge our half-hearted efforts!

Take Advice Carefully and Wisely

You are who you take advice from.

Whatever you do, don't confuse coddling or enabling for support. Don't assume that comfort is a genuine replacement for guidance, or that agreement means you have found clarity or understanding.

Surroundings influence, but advice shapes decisions — and decisions shape lives. The people you allow to guide you, whether intentionally or not, hold quiet power over your direction. So, it's worth asking: Are you letting the right people speak into your life?

It's not that other people are cruel or purposefully trying to undermine you. In fact, people may give us advice from a genuine place of wanting to help. This help, however, may be more accurately understood as a reflection of their own fears, desires, and values, and does not necessarily speak to you.

This does not make them bad or foolish people. But we do need to be aware that people may give us advice that, one way or another, confirms and supports their own choices and interpretations, and helps them make sense of their world. People give advice reflexively, and parrot what they in turn are familiar with, what they believe is being asked for. Many people will scarcely take the time to consider what the "right thing to do" is in the first place, but that won't stop them from telling you.

You can do it. I believe in you. You should follow your heart. Be kind to yourself. Trust your gut. You're doing the best you can.

These platitudes are often offered without thought, and sometimes, support is even offered with a subtle malice that even the advice-giver is not fully conscious of in themselves. They may readily cheer a person into fashion risks, poor romantic choices, problematic business decisions or risky spending behavior that they would never consider for themselves. "Friends" may supply you with just the right justifications you were looking for to abandon your relationship commitments, buy something you don't need, invest in worthless endeavors, or indulge in unhealthy habits. They may be "there for you," but all their presence provides is some version of what we *want*, and not necessarily what we *need*.

The most dangerous advice often comes labelled with the most alluring, innocent-sounding names: Consider the endless variety of self-defeating behaviors modern man has been able to smuggle inside that unassuming term, "self-care."

"I skipped gym again today. I feel so guilty. I'm such a failure."

"Hey, don't say that, you're *not* a failure. You're doing the best you can. You need to learn to go a little easier on yourself."

This is a kind friend. This is a person who cares about you. But what if that sense of guilt is only there precisely because you know deep down that you *haven't*, in fact, been doing the best you can? Unless you have a friend willing to acknowledge that uncomfortable truth, nothing changes. *Feeling* better is not the same as *getting* better.

In real life, the devil doesn't appear to us in a devil costume, complete with horns and a tail. He doesn't say, "Hey there, would you like to come over to the dark side with me and be bad?"

Instead, the temptation he presents really *is* tempting. He invites you to reframe the bad as good. And, in our weakness, we desperately want to believe it. "Hey there, don't you think you're fine just the way you are? Skipping gym is not the end of the world, big deal, why be so uptight about it? It's not your fault, anyway. It's the world's fault. In fact, you're so brave and strong for pushing against all those crazy beauty standards. I'm proud of you."

We can re-imagine the devil, then, not as a blatantly destructive force, but as one that is dangerously supportive, appealing, and encouraging. In our own weakness, we don't ask exactly *what* he is supporting or encouraging.

Emotional support from those who love us is essential. But it's worth recognizing that this is not a replacement for sound guidance, which can only come from those who have additional qualifications — be that experience, wisdom, knowledge, or good sense.

The automatic impulse may be to turn to those closest to us during times of stress and uncertainty. These people can and do help us emotionally. However, they may be completely unable to offer realistic and actionable advice, especially if their own lives are marred by confusion, poor choices, or unconscious habits.

They may love us enormously and want the best for us, but it doesn't automatically follow that they *know* what's best for us. We can love them without loving their mindset, their choices, or their perspective. We can love them without taking on their attitude to life as our own.

The Bottom Line:

If you consistently place yourself in the company of miserable people, you'll absorb their negativity.

If you take advice from those who are undisciplined and unfocused (even if they're "nice"), you'll only learn to excuse your own laziness.

If you depend on people who themselves repeat the same mistakes without learning from them, you'll likely find yourself doing the same.

We do not need to discard people from our lives or get ruthless about who we consider worthy to help us — after all, *we* are the ones in need of guidance. It's not even that we need to strive to follow "successful" people, since those that have failed and grown from the failure often have more wisdom to share than those who never failed.

It takes a kind of wisdom to honestly acknowledge our ignorance, and a kind of discernment to identify those who are most able to lift us out of it.

What is good for your ego is seldom good for your growth.

Chapter 9: Improvement Is Not Keeping Up with the Joneses

Eighteenth century French philosopher Denis Diderot was the author of the most comprehensive Encyclopedia the world had ever seen. Catherine the Great of Russia was so impressed with his work that she offered him a small fortune to purchase his library, instantly ushering Diderot into a more prosperous condition.

In celebration of this new person he had become, he purchased a brand-new scarlet dressing robe — something more fitting of his new station in life — and promptly discarded the old one.

Diderot explains how upon receiving the scarlet robe, his sense of satisfaction quickly gives way to an uncomfortable realization that everything else in his bedroom looks shabby by comparison. He buys a leather chair, but the same thing happens, and soon a cascade of purchases follow: fine curtains, sculptures, ornaments, linens, and fancy imported rugs.

The result of this punishing project of improvement is that Diderot acquires one final unintended possession: debt. Diderot reflects on the experience in an amusing short story titled, "Regrets on Parting with My Old Dressing Gown." Diderot's tale is not really about dressing gowns or Russian Empresses, but about something curious in human nature.

The Diderot Effect

The upward spiral of overconsumption is now well-known to psychologists, and has been variously termed "reactive consumption," getting on the "the hedonic treadmill" or, more classically, "keeping up with the Joneses," except in this case, we're keeping up with an idealized internal concept of our own identity.

This phenomenon is dangerous, but doubly so when we confuse it for personal development and self-improvement. A good question to ask is, "Am I really *improving* here, or am I just caught in a reactive panic, desperately trying to keep up with my own vision of who I think I should be?"

Diderot explains,

> "I was the absolute master of my old dressing gown, but I have become a slave to my new one. Beware of the contamination of sudden wealth. The poor man may take his ease without thinking of appearances, but the rich man is always under a strain."

Diderot uncovered something important about human motivation, dissatisfaction, and the paradoxical ease and fulfilment to be found in simply being content. Perhaps he could have taken his investigation even further, and realized that it was not wealth that was the contaminant, but rather his own idea about how a person with wealth ought to conduct themselves, and how they should live. The money was not the problem. The obligation to play the role of someone with money was the problem.

How are we to discern the difference between genuine incremental improvements in life, and the strain (not just strain but *slavery*) described by Diderot? The outward actions may look the same. The mindset that informs them, however, could not be more different.

Do our choices and actions come from a panicked sense of dissatisfaction, vanity, shame, insufficiency, competitiveness, greed, or ingratitude?

Or are our actions a sincere expression of our readiness to grow?

Diderot purchased more and more material things to "match" the material things he already had. There is nothing aspirational about this, rather, it is a way to "keep up" and attain some ideal vision. There is a psychic tension created when you entertain a mental vision of your ideal self, because you inevitably compare yourself to it, and the comparison is not flattering. Everything in your world that was previously satisfactory suddenly seems lacking, and you feel compelled to *fix* it. Without realizing it, you may get dragged into acquiring all the trappings of the new identity... without legitimately acquiring the identity itself.

We may find that, ironically, making one small "improvement" in life suddenly casts an unflattering light on things on the rest of our lifestyle. The market will happily supply any number of expensive solutions to help us address the creeping sense of dissatisfaction we feel, and before we know it we are not making efforts to be successful people, but rather making efforts to conform to the *image* of a successful person.

Clarify Your Core Intentions

"What am I actually trying to change, and why?"

There was nothing wrong with Diderot's old dressing gown. Had he never entertained the idea of upgrading his lifestyle, he would have continued to be satisfied with it, or perhaps never given it a second thought. Amusingly, there was nothing wrong with the fancy new scarlet dressing gown he purchased, either!

Yet he went on to purchase the next thing, then the next. If he had taken a moment to ask himself the question above, he may have discovered either that the motivation behind these "improvements" was ultimately illegitimate. The irony is that the intention to "play the role of a wealthy person" was precisely the thing that led him straight back to poverty.

Before adding in new habits, tools, ideas, techniques, or routines, anchor yourself in a clear purpose. Not every part of your life needs to change just because one part is changing.

Avoid Overcorrecting

"Am I trying to make a dramatic change or a meaningful one?"

Why a scarlet dressing robe, anyway? Why Persian rugs and leather sofas? In Diderot's mind, these are the kinds of things a wealthy person owns, but does he actually like these things? In reality, they may not connect meaningfully to his actual values, habits, or lifestyle. They do not supply any genuine pleasure beyond ticking an arbitrary box.

Prior to coming into money, Diderot had lived in relative poverty. The scarlet robe is thus a symbol not just of his overcorrection of the problem, but of doing so in a generic way that bears no connection to the facts of his life. It's like accurately acknowledging the problem of a poor diet, but then overcorrecting by adopting the identity of an extreme vegan raw-food enthusiast who regularly fasts for three days at a time.

Growth doesn't have to be dramatic to count. Changes should be realistic and appropriate. A change may be big and flashy, but if it's not connected meaningfully to our values, our goals, and our actual lives, then the change is likely to be shallow and fleeting.

Instead of throwing yourself into drastic overnight transformations, have the discipline to be content with one small change at a time. Pause. Give that change time to percolate into the rest of your life. Give your identity time to adjust and adapt. Try to ignore how the outward expression of a change *looks to other people* and focus on how that change *feels to you*.

Measure Progress by Consistency, Not Aesthetics

Looking disciplined is not the same as being disciplined. Tens of thousands of successful social media influencers make their living selling the *illusion* of a perfect life. This does not require them to know anything about that life, or be actively living it themselves. In fact, the industry works better when you don't attain this perfect life either, so that you continue to return and keep buying the same product — the illusion — from them over and over again.

Cultivate a preference for the real thing, not the glossy appearance of the thing. You can be a successful artist without the high-end art supplies and Instagram-worthy art studio. You can be fit, strong, and healthy without the on-trend workout clothing. You can be a highly effective and driven entrepreneur without a color-coded calendar, a perfect desk setup, or a library of self-help books.

What matters is that you're taking conscious steps towards your commitments, day after day. What matters is that you're consistently showing up and *doing the work*. Let go of any idealized image of how that work is supposed to look — that's a distraction.

The Bottom Line:

Am I making real changes to my life or am I just doing what I think people do when they change?

The world is ready to offer us millions of images of what a successful, disciplined, and effective person looks like. Think carefully if you want these images.

It's better to be the master of change in your life, and not its slave.

To be truly ambitious, desire the real thing.

Chapter 10: Put Your Commitments in Black and White

There is power and magic in the written word.

Wanting things, claiming things, planning for things... all of this is formless until it is captured and calcified in a written word.

For our species, the history of written language has always been the history of certification, accuracy, authority, ownership, and influence. It is the medium of binding promises and pledges.

It is why we commemorate any solemn and binding claim with great ceremonies around the setting down of terms, and the signing of signatures. Mariage certificates, contracts, treatises, the law... if a thing is important, it is set down in black and white.

It should be that way with our own commitments to ourselves.

Write Down Your Goals

The 1979, researchers asked new graduates from the Harvard MBA program whether they wrote down clear goals for their future plans. They found that 87% of students didn't have specific goals at all, 13% had goals but didn't write them down, and just 3% had goals and had also committed them to paper.

Ten years later, the researchers discovered that the 13% of graduates who had goals were earning twice as much as those without goals, and the 3% with written goals were earning ten times as much as everyone else.

Understandably, these results were rapidly proliferated across countless personal development blogs, business coaching articles, and the LinkedIn pages of productivity gurus and entrepreneurs. One major drawback of "The Harvard Study," however, was that it never existed, except perhaps as a neat demonstration of how misinformation can spread.

However, the bogus study does point to a legitimate phenomenon. The real evidence for the power of written goals comes from Dr. Gail Matthews, a psychology professor at Dominican University of California. Her

2007 study investigated the different possible approaches to goal setting, and how they influence success.

First, 267 participants were randomly assigned to one of five groups:

- Goals not written
- Goals written
- Goals written plus action commitments
- Goals written plus action commitments to a friend
- Goals written plus action commitments and progress reports to a friend

Though all the participants worked on a wide variety of goals, the results at the end of the study showed that those in the final group achieved more than all the other groups. The researchers discovered that it was not merely a question of written goal vs. unwritten goal, but rather that written goals were especially powerful when combined with accountability and public commitment.

Write Down Your Goals

Make them as clear and specific as possible and physically write them down by hand to reinforce the idea that you are putting down a binding promise to yourself. You might like to literally format this document as a contract or certificate. Sign it. Display it somewhere visible.

Commit to Taking Action

The written goal should increase your sense of urgency, not decrease it. Allow the goal to inform precise practical steps to take, in sequence. Your plan doesn't have to be perfect, but you should at least have a clear idea of the very next move you need to make.

Tell Someone

A private promise is easier to break than a public one. Increase the likelihood of follow-through by making your intentions known to someone else. Choose someone who you will feel uncomfortable admitting a broken commitment to.

Track Your Progress Weekly, and Report Back

Consistently reflect on where you are in the process and always be mindful of your position relative to your stated goal and intention. Check with your accountability friend not just to confirm that you are staying the path, but also to offer a report of how you've done so. This is a powerful opportunity to reflect, adjust, and celebrate any gains.

The Bottom Line:

Are you really committed to your goals?

Honor your own words.

Commitment means staying loyal to what you said you'd do long after the mood you said it in has passed. When you write something down, it takes on a concreteness, which acts to hold you accountable, no matter what. Putting an idea down into words makes it real; it is the very first step we take to bring the entire idea to life in the real world.

Put your promises to yourself down in black and white.

Chapter 11: Don't Be Wasteful of Your Time

The phrase "wasting time" is so ubiquitous that you may have never given it much thought. When you *do* give it thought, it quickly starts to seem a little strange — time simply flows at the rate it flows, and everyone moves through it in an identical way. If two people both wake up at 8am, exactly twelve hours later both will be in the same place — 8pm. How could either of them have "wasted" any of those twelve hours?

It is more accurate to talk about what we ourselves do in and with those twelve hours. Certainly, time passes regardless, but our *effort* can be inelegant, misguided, and wasteful.

Parkinson's Law

Cyril Northcote Parkinson wrote a funny article for *The Economist* in 1955. In this article he tells the story of a woman who has just one thing to do today — send a postcard.

While this is a task that would take any busy person two minutes to accomplish, this woman takes a more leisurely approach and finds a way to draw out every step of the process so that it fills the entire day that's available to her.

She takes the long route to walk to the post office, then takes her time carefully selecting the postcard, then even more time choosing a stamp, then painstakingly dawdles with message itself, and on and on...

Parkinson's Law is as follows: "Work expands to fill the time available for its completion."

In this sense, the woman is wasteful — she spends a full day on a task that doesn't require it. Every minute she spends on the task beyond the purely necessary two minutes is in essence wasted. Yet, the woman may say at the end of the day that she was busy, and in a certain way, she was.

The trick of Parkinson's law is to understand precisely what wasted time *looks* like — it does not look like someone sitting on the sofa doing nothing. It looks like a flustered woman busying herself with an air of importance as she bustles around and does a series of active yet ultimately worthless tasks. Wasted time is not inactivity — it is activity spent for nothing.

If you give yourself all week to finish something, that's precisely how long the task will take... even if it only ever needed two hours. All the while you are drawing out the task and filling your time, you may relax in the illusion that you are busy. But are you?

Discipline requires not just that we take action and complete tasks, but that we adhere to self-imposed structure and limits. Without them, a kind of bloat and shapelessness sets in, we lose sight of our priorities, and our momentum dribbles away. Worse still, we may congratulate ourselves for staying busy. Some of the world's most masterful timewasters are those that give a very convincing appearance of busyness.

Don't assume motion is progress.

Train yourself to respect time and use it elegantly and wisely. Place time limits on yourself, cut the fluff, and stay focused. Busy work can be a deadly distraction and diversion; over time, you may even teach yourself to require more and more time to do less and less. Setting your sights low and then falling short even of those is a surefire path to demoralization and a feeling of ineptitude.

Timebox Everything

If work expands to fill the time allotted to it, then allocate *less* time to it, and you will paradoxically have more time on your hands. There is never any need to rush, of course, but be mindful about what clean, focused action feels like.

Set short, specific deadlines for every task. Even if you are under no external time limit, have the discipline to impose one on yourself. Instead of saying, "I'll write this today," say, "I'll finish this draft by 11 a.m." If you don't, you may find that you've unconsciously given yourself permission to take the entire day to write… plus some of tomorrow. Nothing seems to get done when you have all the time in the world. Instead, a little time pressure brings clarity and forces you to be productive.

Use a Weekly Completion Cycle

Find a rhythm. At the beginning of every week, clearly mark out the work you intend to do and when you intend to do it, then at the end of the week, pause to reflect and see how you fared. Taking the time to acknowledge how much you've accomplished builds self-respect. You are allowing yourself to build up a realistic and proactive sense of just what you are capable of given your time resources.

Routinely revisiting your goals and intentions also gives you a chance to put to bed outstanding projects and tasks that have outlived their relevance and would only distract and delay you if you didn't deliberately divest your attention from them and put it elsewhere.

Anchor Your Requests and Plans to Time

Taking conscious responsibility for how you will use your time has the side effect of encouraging clearer, more intentional language. Instead of, "I'll do this soon," commit to putting more shape and structure to your claims: "I'll send this over at noon tomorrow." That subtle shift creates urgency and accountability.

If you struggle with procrastination, being more precise and time-anchored with your language can create more calm and clarity. Instead of being haunted by a nebulous cloud of open but ill-defined tasks, you can set clear targets for yourself and clearly identify when they have or haven't been achieved. You have plucked yourself out of the stressful cloud and can come back down again to earth. Here, time is not some loose, abstract concept, but rather a fixed and measurable thing that you can handle in concrete, predictable ways.

The Bottom Line:

Parkinson's law tells us that "Work expands to fill the time available for its completion." The antidote for this form of time wasting is the discipline of self-imposed time limits.

Identify what's most important, set a reasonable time frame in which to do it, then get to work.

If you don't waste it, there is always enough time for things that matter.

Chapter 12: It's Not Clever, It's Complicated

There are two tools in front of you. One has loads of buttons, dials, wires, and tubes, and comes with a novel-sized instruction manual. The other is far simpler, and its instructions fit on one side of a business card.

There is something in human nature that believes that the first tool is more sophisticated, more powerful, and more intelligent in some way. However, this is an illusion. The more time you spend managing and maintaining the tool itself, the less time there is to actually use the tool, and the less useful it is overall.

The value of a tool, then, is not in how complex it is, but in how much unnecessary complexity it removes from our lives.

An organizational system is a kind of tool. Try to avoid the trap of introducing a tool that demands more of you than it gives. For example, you waste time setting up a time management system, or you get carried away organizing your organization system itself, rather than your life.

A startling but obvious fact: A complicated productivity system is not what makes us more productive. A complicated note-taking system is not what makes us diligent and knowledgeable. A complicated discipline system is not what makes us disciplined.

Ultimately, being productive, diligent, and disciplined comes down to a series of actions and a set of attitudes wholly independent of any system you might wish to design around it.

Why set up a system that is more complicated than it needs to be?

The answer is fear. We are afraid that we cannot do what we want to do without the system, and so that system becomes a kind of lucky charm, a magic talisman that if we can just keep focusing on, will allow us to achieve what we want. If we fail or fall short, we can blame the system and reassure ourselves that if we only make this or that adjustment, we'll do better next time. The system gets more complex. But we don't get any braver or more resolute.

Whether your system is simple or complex, one thing is always true: at some point, you need to act. You need to overcome resistance, do the terrifying thing, or face the unknown.

Get rid of the idea that the only thing standing in your way is discovering the perfect productivity system, once and for all. Do not confuse complexity for cleverness. If you find yourself overcomplicating the system itself, ask yourself what you may be avoiding. If your answer is "the actual work" then be brave and face the fact that the discomfort of doing new and difficult things never goes away. You can tinker with to-do lists and endlessly reorganize your apps and software, but when you're done, the intimidating task is still there, unchanged and waiting.

According to Parkinson's law, we often allow tasks to bloat and bulge and take up any and all time when we are not disciplined enough. We can imagine a similar principle: distractions expand to match our avoidance and fear. How do you know you're done with a task that you never needed to do in the first place?

Say No to Unnecessary Complexity

An alternative to complex systems: Make one list.

Every task goes onto it. Each day, pick a few tasks to focus on, and do only those. At the end of the day, think about what you'd like to do about those tasks that didn't get done.

The next day, repeat the process.

No need for multiple phone or desktop apps, no need for a convoluted notebook system, and no need to fritter away time on figuring how to get all your notebooks and apps to sync up.

If you feel a pang of apprehension at the idea of such a simple system, become curious about that fear. Such a simple list forces you to drop the busy work and just get started on what matters. Your focus shifts to the task itself and away from the tool — which you can no longer hide behind. The smaller and simpler the list, the less of a buffer there is between you and concrete action. That's a good thing.

It is always better to start with a system and adjust it *down* to meet your genuine needs, rather than picking an overly complex system and adjusting yourself *up* to meet its complexity.

Complicated systems stem from fear, but they also create fear.

A long and complicated system creates the impression that it's *needed* — that the problem it is there to solve is also complicated. We look at all the levers and pulleys, all the steps, all the different apps and tools, and we mistakenly think that we need to use all of them. This can feel overwhelming and intimidating, and subtly our loyalties shift from the task itself to the appeasement of the great complicated beast that supposedly enables the completion of that task.

A complex system that shows you a bigger picture than you need to see can be intimidating. You can only do one thing at a time, and you can only do so many things in the limited number of hours you have in the day. So why stress yourself out planning and re-planning all the countless steps and components that you can't tackle yet, instead of focusing on what you can accomplish?

Tomorrow is another day, and with it you make another updated list that considers what you've achieved today. Procrastination and anxiety are often panic responses because we are overly focused on the size and complexity of the entire task, instead of focusing on the simplicity and immediacy of the one or two things that we can handle right now, today.

The Bottom Line:

Choose tools and habits that make your life simpler, not more complex. Don't waste time mastering or managing a complex productivity system that won't bring any more benefits than a simple one.

Choose tools that make action more likely, not less.

Thinking will not overcome fear, but action will.

Chapter 13: Don't Forfeit Growth for Comfort

The brain has evolved a sophisticated threat-detection mechanism that has successfully protected our species for hundreds of thousands of years. Fear is a visceral trigger to remove ourselves as quickly and effectively as possible from what appears to be dangerous. The reward for fleeing that fear is a sense of calm relief… and comfort.

However, there is no matching human emotion that spurs us *out* of that comfort once we've landed there. There is no irresistible force that will kick in and inspire us to strive for excellence. No organism on earth innately overextends itself once it is adequately safe, fed, and warm. For many people, the comfort itself is the reward and the goal. So long as there is no real danger and needs are met, what's the problem?

The problem is that there *is* a cost to staying in the comfort zone, but it's hidden from us. The cost we pay is the growth we could have experienced. While coasting along in mediocrity, we may not feel as though we're in any real danger, and few people will bother to push themselves. That's precisely what makes mediocrity so very hazardous.

Getting trapped in "OK, but not great." is a far greater risk than outright failure and is more common. At least failure might be accurately called failure — the lukewarm liminal space that is neither success nor failure, however, just feels like nothing.

When you stay in "OK," you train your brain to accept and expect the status quo. That then becomes your baseline. You may stop wondering what lies beyond the baseline, and whatever potential you may have had rusts from lack of use. You forget that more might have been possible.

Don't Settle for Mediocrity

By rewarding your comfort, you teach yourself to enjoy and attach to that comfort, and so you're less willing to part with it when invited to, even a little. What felt comfortable some years ago now feels a little scant, since your life has not kept pace with your development and maturation. Any fresh goals, desires, and dreams languish and lose their urgency because you consider the fulfilment of your prior goals and dreams sufficient.

In this state of mind, your actions and perspectives are rewarding comfort but actively discouraging growth. You may not even register the full implication of this until it's too late. One day you might notice that for all your comfort, you are not in any way *excited*. Perhaps you no longer feel quite so alive. Having carefully removed from life the sting of the unknown, you may discover that certain other things have been lost along with it.

It's not taboo to relax. To find contentment, peace, and gratitude for exactly where you are is a natural part of life. But it cannot be *all* of life. To make that rest and enjoyment sweet, to make it meaningful, it needs to occur alongside growth, learning, exploration, maturation, risk-taking, and challenge.

It's not that we shouldn't rest, reflect, or recuperate, but rather that we should not fill our days with low-stakes tasks that ultimately lead nowhere. We should stay alert and never allow "good enough" to be the highest we can imagine from ourselves.

Set a Deadline for Your Excuses

It's human nature to construct a running narrative about who you are, what is possible for you, and why you do the things you do. The first step to making changes to your actual life, however, is making changes to *the story you tell about that life*. You have to drop all the excuses and justifications.

"It's not the right time."

"I'm exhausted."

"I'll do it just as soon as…"

Be honest with yourself. If you consistently heard these same excuses from an employee, for example, would you accept them as legitimate? Excuses stay in place because they're comfortable and easy. Some of our excuses may be extremely convincing and even flattering; we may genuinely fool ourselves into thinking that it's someone or something else's fault. How could I possibly do that course when I'm already rushed off my feet taking care of everyone else? They won't let me have a minute!

Look your excuses in the eye and let them know they have a shelf life. Set a deadline for yourself. If time, energy, or money is an obstacle, take action to remove it from your path rather than getting comfortable with the fact that it's in your way. You don't need to have a full, perfect plan to begin. Simply agree with yourself to no longer let fear, hesitation, laziness, or self-delusion run the show.

Take Baby Steps

Personal development is not an extreme sport. Being courageous simply means teaching yourself to disregard fear as the main driving force of your life. Pushing yourself to confront fear without challenging the thought patterns beneath it is more or less masochism and is not necessary.

If you can take small, consistent steps towards the things that matter, and resist the small, daily temptations to relax to a lower standard, over time you *will* thrive, with no need for dramatic overnight transformations or heroic "cold turkey" moments. Don't let your fear and resistance make the next step seem bigger and more intimidating than it is. Small, humble efforts compound over time.

Make "Comfort" Uncomfortable

Mediocrity sets in because it feels so pleasant and easy. One way to break this motivational inertia is to consciously make this kind of mediocrity *less* comfortable, and *less* easy. Surround yourself with proactive people who prompt you to keep moving and growing, i.e., people who will make your own inertia and laxity stand out all the more obviously.

Engineer your routine so that you must take steps to opt out of commitments, rather than making the default state one of no action. Book a gym class up front that will cost you money and a little embarrassment to cancel. Be aware of your favorite excuse and make it literally impossible to resort to. For example, "I only binge on overpriced junk food in the evening because I just don't have time to cook" is an excuse that won't hold water if you have a freezer full of nutritious, pre-prepared meals. You may still make an undisciplined choice, but this way, you cannot hide behind the excuse. And that will be uncomfortable.

The Bottom Line:

Is the ease and comfort I feel right now *really* better than the potential growth I could have if only I was a little braver and more disciplined?

Leaving our comfort zone can feel awkward, frightening, and unpleasant, while staying small can feel safe and cozy. But our feelings are not always an accurate reflection of the value of certain actions; feeling fear doesn't automatically mean we are doing something dangerous, nor does feeling comfort mean that we are doing something harmless.

Fear shrinks your world. Courage expands it.

Chapter 14: Am I Being Productive or Just Frantic?

When it comes to action, *quantity* is not a substitute for *quality*.

An action is a high-quality one if it connects meaningfully to a relevant goal, and achieves that goal efficiently, i.e., maximum impact using minimum resources.

Multiplying the number of irrelevant, low-impact, or wasteful activities may only give a superficial impression of productivity.

Multitasking Doesn't Work

More correctly, multitasking doesn't exist. The term itself betrays a misconception — there is no real way to conduct more than one effortful task at the same time. Instead, the multitasker is actually switching rapidly between one task and another, and every switch comes with an attentional cost.

According to Dr. Gloria Mark (Chancellor's Professor of Informatics at UC Irvine and author of *Attention Span*) every time you shift your attention, your brain pays a "reset" cost, which takes time, increases mistakes, and drains your mental energy. It's like not being able to swim and run track at the same time. You could certainly *try* to swim a lap, get out the pool, towel off, change into running gear, jog once around the field, put your swimsuit back on, get into the pool, do another lap, and so on. You'd be constantly moving, but so much of that movement would be unnecessary "switching." It would be easier to work through one task until completion, then move to the next.

Multitasking not only fails to make you more productive, it also actively hinders your productivity. Constant task-switching raises stress levels, making you feel mentally scattered. Your engagement with the tasks is shallow and rushed, and even as you're frantic, there's an anxious feeling that things are not quite in control. You're bringing more chaos into the tasks than exists there naturally, inviting overwhelm and stress that simply doesn't need to be there.

Cut the Noise

It's easy to slip into multitasking when it seems like the only option. We may be in the habit of dutifully responding to everything in our environment that claims to be urgent, but is it really? Is the clock really ticking, and are all these tasks as necessary and essential as they seem?

Dr. Mark recommends removing any potential triggers that prompt this kind of panicked, unthinking response and the belief that we need to multitask to keep up. Turn off email notifications, put your phone on silent or out of sight and reach, and set limits on what you allow to spontaneously intrude into your conscious awareness. These constant pings pull your brain in different directions, demand your attention, and create the false impression that they are owed a reaction in the first place.

Fewer interruptions mean fewer chances for your focus to shatter. Proactively decide when you are going to read emails or respond to messages and guard the rest of your time from digital intrusions.

Monotask with Intention

Focus on one mentally demanding task at a time and commit a solid chunk of prolonged effort to accomplishing it. Your brain takes time to settle into a task, but if you can avoid fracturing your attention before it settles in this way, you will gradually gain more mental momentum and sink into a state of *deep work*.

Do as much as you can in one go. If your allocated task time is up but you're deeply engrossed, don't stop. Marathon runners can fall into a groove, a kind of flow state where their mind is totally focused, their muscles are warm and limber, and it feels almost as if stopping would take more effort than continuing. The same can happen with mental effort, if we are diligent enough to stay warmed up and in motion.

When it is time to stop, identify a natural "breakpoint" in the work, like the end of a paragraph or section. This is a way to stay psychologically neat and cut down on the mess and inelegance of dropping in and out of tasks at random places. Pick a place to stop so that, when you next work on the task, there is as little startup cost as possible, and you can easily pick up where you left off.

Take a Real Break Between Tasks

Your brain needs time to reset to baseline before diving into the next activity. We are not machines; we need to warm up into a new task, and we need to wind down when we're done. Overlapping tasks or scheduling them too close to one another may feel like it's saving time, but you are only ensuring that those warm-up and cool-down periods eat into what should be deep, productive work.

It's like throwing yourself onto the running track while you're still flustered and damp from swimming. You're technically on track, but you're also rattled and unfocused. You may inadvertently undermine your entire run by starting out in such a frazzled and reactive way.

Instead, Dr. Mark suggests short, intentional breaks to settle and gather yourself after completing a work session. Give your body time to release tension, and your brain time to disengage. Step outside, stretch and walk around for a moment, get a drink, have a quick chat or listen to a podcast. Dedicating just a few moments to reset and rebalance in this way will help you to show up to your next work session with a calm, unencumbered mind.

The Bottom Line:

Multitasking is an effective way to multiply stress and friction, and to divide and dilute your power and energy until it's worthless.

Multitasking is a problem posing as a solution; multitasking is distraction.

Chapter 15: Every Yes Is a No, Every No Is a Yes

Yes is the positive word, and *no* is the negative one. Or is it?

Every time you say *yes* to something you don't want or need, you're simultaneously saying no to something else that really matters — your wellbeing, your priorities, or your peace and quiet.

A boundary can be understood as a kind of yes/no pair. A boundary is like a little fence set up around something of value; when you assert that something *doesn't* belong inside the fence, you are simultaneously making a positive claim about what *does* belong.

Say No

It's difficult, though, when the word "no" carries so much emotional baggage. We live in a world of people who are hostile to the concept of limits and restrictions in general, and to the concept of not getting their way in particular. Many of us behave as though an obstacle to getting what we want is more or less an affront to our basic human freedom, and are primed to view any "no" as invalid and essentially up for negotiation.

The other side of this coin is the sinking feeling that our own "no" is never quite warranted, and that to refuse someone's request is to inconvenience them, disappoint them, or otherwise volunteer yourself as an unwanted obstacle in their plans and desires.

So we say yes.

We agree to do things that we don't have the time for, take on responsibility for things we don't really care about, or acquiesce to things that later make us feel compromised.

However, saying no to a request is not necessarily rude or selfish, and what's more, saying yes to a request is not necessarily kind or helpful.

The most effective, balanced, and productive people are those that know they can do anything, but they can't do everything. While discipline is often framed as the attempt to harness one's attention and energy and direct it to the thing that matters most, there is also a corresponding skill of consciously withdrawing that same attention and energy away from the things that don't matter.

The most productive and effective person says no far, far more often than they say yes. They are selective and intentional, pouring all of themselves into what counts, and skipping the rest. It's not even that we need to devalue the things we deliberately say no to, only that we need to be keenly aware of something we may value much more. If you would have enough of your resources to invest in one amazing idea, then you need the discipline to refrain from wasting those resources on a thousand good ideas.

Pause Before You Answer

A request is not an obligation or an order.

The moment of receiving a request we don't want to or can't fulfil can be awkward, but don't try to reduce the tension by hurrying to say yes. Even if a person's request is framed as urgent for *them personally*, remember that doesn't mean that it is an emergency for *you*.

Buy yourself time by answering, "I'll check my calendar first," or "Let me get back to you." This gives you space to remove yourself from any immediate sense of pressure or obligation, and reflect carefully on where this request actually fits in, given your priorities and limits.

Ask the Right Questions

Someone may ask if you'll volunteer to organize an extensive school field trip in six months' time for five dozen kids. You might ask yourself, "Do I want to volunteer for this in six months' time?" but it may be smarter to reframe the question as, "If I had to fulfil this request *today*, would I still agree to it?"

If you can't in all honesty answer "Yes!" to this question, then it's not reasonable to assume that the future will somehow be different.

Remember that you are always at liberty to decide the extent to which you can accommodate a request.

Their request may be, "Can you volunteer to organize the school trip?" But it doesn't have to be a yes or a no. You can ask yourself, "How much am I willing to help here? What would I be comfortable doing?"

Thinking in this way shifts your focus away from reacting to what others expect of you, and onto proactively identifying what you are willing to do. This puts you in charge.

"I likely won't have time to organize the whole trip, but I can pitch in for the gas, and I'm happy to book a bus for everyone."

Say No Kindly but Clearly

Guilt at being the bad guy may make you present your own reasonable refusal as something unfortunate, misguided, or unfair. The quickest way to communicate to other people that we don't take our own boundaries all that seriously is to apologize profusely when we assert them, then rush to offer a consolation prize. What's more, following up a polite refusal with endless explanations and justifications has the effect of making the refusal feel more impolite, and more suspect. Even worse, you may accidentally invite less perceptive people to argue and negotiate with you.

"Oh, I'm afraid I can't. I wish I could, but my dog is sick, and I can't leave him at home today!"

"Oh, no problem. Just bring your dog!"

Finally, internalize the fact that you don't owe anyone an apology or lengthy explanation. You don't need to ask permission to say no, nor do you need to offer up something else to make up for your refusal. Simply be warm and polite: "Thank you for the invitation, but I don't have time to devote to that right now."

Less is more. Remind yourself that protecting your time and energy does not mean that you are rejecting that person, or that you don't care about them or what they're doing; it simply means that you are honoring your priorities.

Consider What You DO Owe People

Is our unwilling acquiescence *really* useful to other people?

Do we *really* do anyone any favors by "helping" them purely out of guilt?

Do our friends and loved ones *really* require us to deplete ourselves?

Do not willfully violate your own boundaries and then act as though you have been pressed into it by someone else. An insincere *yes* introduces an energy of guilt and obligation that the requester themselves may not want. A genuine *no*, on the other hand, can strengthen relationships and build trust. It makes our *yes* more trustworthy and meaningful when we do give it.

Think carefully about what you actually owe others. People-pleasers are seldom respected or cherished for their compliance. Instead, your own authenticity, self-respect, and integrity may ultimately be of more value in your relationships than your self-sacrifice, your burnout, or your passivity.

The Bottom Line:

Discipline is a two-sided coin: one side is focused, diligent action taken towards the things we care most about; the other side is the ability to say no everything else.

People are entitled to make requests, and you are entitled to refuse them, and neither person is doing anything wrong.

On the other side of "no, thank you," is everything you want to say "yes" to.

Chapter 16: Master Long-Term Thinking

You pick up your phone and the second the blast of pixelated blue light hits your retinas, you forget why you picked it up in the first place (there was no reason other than blind, conditioned habit). Your finger starts to scroll and poke the screen automatically (again, habit) as you dig around the same old informational water holes you've become most accustomed to visiting.

In no time you're plugged into a stream, as seemingly endless novelty presents itself to your consideration as though on a conveyor belt. You allow yourself to be quietly lulled, the algorithms steering you this way and that way by your own reactivity.

But the "infinite" scroll is a misnomer. There is nothing infinite here; instead, this kind of mindlessness imprisons you in a permanent, ever-refreshing moment that doesn't connect to the past or the future in any meaningful way. Eventually, you put your phone aside. Time has passed. But what has been achieved?

Today we live in a short-term world. Too many of our responses are pre-conditioned, mindless, and automatic. We are reactive and impulsive. Without knowing it, many of us have no strategy beyond paying attention to what is immediately in our field of awareness. We have an internal "infinite scroll," and we distract ourselves.

In a world filled with instant gratification, decisions are made *now*, to get results *now*. Our attention spans shrink along with our vision, along with any real understanding of how our actions in the present may meaningfully connect to the future.

Long-term thinking, on the other hand, is indistinguishable from self-discipline and from focused strategy. Thinking with a view to the future gives you a broader vision. You see not just what's in front of you, but how those things may change and evolve with time. You see how your actions can't be judged solely by what they yield in the now, but where they take you a day, a week, or a month from now.

Discipline Is the Long Game

Whatever it is that you might want in the future, the time to start working towards that is today, right here and right now. Long-term thinking is the *why*, and grit, determination, and discipline are the *how*. What would happen if every action you took in the present was not mindless and reactive, but dedicated? In other words, what if every action was spoken for, and connected in clear ways to a future goal?

Without self-discipline, long-term goals will always be just fantasy. Without long-term thinking, even self-discipline becomes punishment without purpose.

When you can think far ahead, you can act far ahead, too. This requires patience, courage, and realistic expectations — i.e., mature awareness of the fact that the time between setting a goal and achieving that goal can be long. Very long.

Self-discipline is the ability to stay on course, no matter what temptations or distractions emerge in the meantime. It means refusing to let random chance, luck, other people's preferences or your own lazy or addictive habits steer your life. You don't get swept up. Instead, your actions are deliberately connected to the results you intend for yourself and are set apart for that purpose.

The tricky thing is that sometimes, it's the short-term thinking we are most rewarded for — at least in the short-term. We need to consistently push against what is rote and predictable, what feels safe and easy right now, and instead keep our eyes on work that consistently builds our future — even if we are the only ones who can see that future right now.

Your most intelligent, optimal, and disciplined move in this moment may not look like much or bring you any instant rewards. Doing the disciplined thing may be distinctly ungratifying, unpopular, hard, and a little boring at times. But have faith in the power of exponential growth.

Any worthless, fleeting thing can give you a feel-good rush in the moment. But then, that's all it can ever give you. It will not help when one day you arrive at your supposed future and discover how few of your actions have prepared you for it, and how little you have to show for the time passed.

Time Travel Weekly

Set aside just fifteen minutes every week to have an honest discussion with your future self. This may feel weird and a little unreal, but, misfortunes aside, that future self *will* materialize one day. You get to choose what that future looks like. That choice happens now.

Visualize yourself one, five or even ten years into the future. If you're a long-term thinking novice, simply envision yourself a week from now.

What do you look like, how are you feeling, and what are you doing? Imagine that you have accomplished your goal. Now ask yourself, "Self, what did you do in the past to get where you are now?" Perhaps, what *didn't* you do?

Let this future version of yourself be your mentor and yardstick. Compare your actions in the present against this endpoint — do they bring you closer or further away? When you have tunnel-vision and focus too much on the short-term, it's tempting to weigh up choices against only the most immediate facts of a situation (such as how satisfying an action feels right now). But long after all of that has faded, then what?

Self-discipline gets a whole lot easier when it's grounded in who you're becoming. Look beyond what feels good right now. Hold that vision in your mind's eye as you set tasks for yourself.

Swap Dopamine Hits for Legacy Moves

Try to replace one small instant-gratification habit (scrolling, shopping, snoozing) with a habit that proactively builds equity in your future. Don't rank any single action purely on how appealing it seems in the here and now. Play that choice out and see what dividends it pays in five minutes, in a few days, in a few years. Be real — it *will* feel like a loss to deny yourself that immediate buzz. The disciplined mind can recognize the pleasure in that temptation, but nevertheless see clearly that it pales in comparison to the real prize of building something in sure, lasting increments. Your ROI will be slow... but massive.

Train yourself to find gratification and satisfaction in making sounder investments in yourself, and in your future. For example, keep books in places you'd normally reach for your phone, and read a few pages instead of wasting time on social media. Consciously remind yourself of what this choice means.

Celebrate the fact that you've taken a tiny step *forward*, instead of wasting time on a pleasant but worthless distraction.

Track Progress Like a Scientist, Not a Judge

The most resilient people in the world hold this attitude: "I'm not failing, I'm running experiments."

Long-term thinking is the skill of zooming out and looking at the bigger perspective. They don't tell stories about their own victimhood or unworthiness, but are guided simply by curiosity and the desire to optimize. Daily slip ups are far easier to overcome if you interpret them in the context of overall weekly success.

The Bottom Line:

Think long-term, act short-term.

Track what's working and make intelligent adjustments without getting immobilized by shame and blame. In the end, self-judgment, too, is just a distraction and delay.

Don't give up what you want most for what you want now.

Chapter 17: Understand Controlled, Intentional Risk

Exposing yourself to the possibility of danger — taking a risk — sounds like an obviously unwise thing to do. That danger is only half the picture – the *other* half is that by taking risks, we also expose ourselves to the possibility of growth and gain.

Having low risk tolerance may feel like a safe default position to take. But if we're talking about probabilities, relentlessly resisting change may well be the riskiest thing you can ever do.

Do you have to be a blowhard, all-or-nothing risk-taker who is constantly jeopardizing stability for the *chance* of a good outcome? Thankfully, no. We all vary in our psychological constitution and personal preferences around engaging with the unknown. In fact, things like upbringing, culture, and even hormone levels may impact our risk-taking behavior.

Not all risk is created equal, and just because you "do one thing every day that scares you" does not mean that success is guaranteed. The goal is not to indiscriminately increase risk, but to be more intentional of why and how you're choosing to take those risks. The idea is to cultivate strategic and controlled risk. This takes a high level of self-control and discipline, because it requires consciously overriding your brain's deeply ingrained self-preservation instincts. Taking risks requires you to find the courage to do something that may not be met with approval, to abandon comfort and predictability, and have enough faith in your long-term vision that you are willing to bet your temporary security on it.

You're Not Calculating Risk, You're Down-Regulating Fear

Exposure to the unknown means we simultaneously expose ourselves to potential gain and to potential loss. The rational mind says that we should take that gamble if the potential gain looks like it outweighs the potential loss. This makes sense mathematically, but seldom plays out this way in real life, precisely because the nature of risk is its very uncertainty. You don't know what the chances of risk or reward are. So you're afraid.

Fighting this fear, and not merely running a cost-benefit analysis, is what strategic risk-taking is all about. You may have already done all the mental calculations, and run over the "logical" next step a thousand times in your mind. But if fear is in control, then ultimately you will not be able to reason yourself into taking a strategic and controlled risk.

Of course, toxic positivity and gaslighting yourself into thinking that you can't fail are just as bad catastrophizing. One picture of courage is a warrior entering battle with clenched teeth and fists, another is a conceited startup entrepreneur acting on hype and delusion.

But there's a more reasonable, practical middle ground. We can simply open our eyes to the need to regulate our kneejerk fear response, rewire maladaptive inner narratives, drop unhelpful learned patterns and behaviors, and calmly but surely choose growth over comfort — given the information we have right now. That's *regulated* courage.

Train for Risk Like a Muscle

Smart risk-taking and bravery usually looks nothing like in the movies. Instead of scaring yourself with visions of a looming quantum leap, get busy doing the hard work of small steps today.

Discipline is not a mood. It's a choice. One that does not depend in any way on how you're feeling.

Don't wait until you are feeling bold and inspired. It's a fallacy that certain actions require us to feel certain emotions first. We can act, right now, regardless of how we feel. Often, real boldness is in the immediacy of our action, not its size. Take a small step in the right direction without giving yourself time to argue. Ask a question in that scary meeting, share an opinion, assert a boundary, or make an offer.

Every such tiny act is like a rep that strengthens and trains the courage muscle. In time, overriding your brain's overprotective fear mechanisms will become more and more natural. That's self-discipline: doing the thing before your fear can stop you.

Silence the Catastrophe Narrator

When we are disciplined, we respect and acknowledge our own feelings, but they are not ultimately in charge of what we do day to day. In the same way, we are aware of our thought processes and perceptions, but we don't automatically give them credence.

The thought, "I'm going to fail and destroy my entire life if I act now." may be true, and it may not be. The truth may be some other third thing not yet even considered. The only way to find out is to pause, relax, and seek evidence. Step outside both thoughts and emotions and reconnect to the available facts, your purpose, and your will to achieve that purpose.

The fearful mind wants to help and will do so by violently drawing your attention to worst-case scenarios. Thank it for this life affirming power — it's what kept your ancient ancestors alive. Look at the horror show it's presenting and ask yourself, "Ok, so what? Then what happens?"

Allow your mind to travel "beyond the car crash." Is failing here life-and-death, or is it just embarrassment? Are you in real danger, or are you merely facing the possibility of discomfort? Just because you are perceiving threat, is the threat genuine? And even if there is, might this be a threat that feels like the end of the world in the mind... but is surprisingly more manageable out in the real world.

You don't have to shut that inner voice up completely. This isn't a battle. But one way to lessen the emotional weight of that voice is to consciously consider the best-case scenario, too. Complete the "What if...?" with unexpected boom, not doom, and see how you feel about taking the risk.

Channel Curiosity Instead of Control

Your brain needs direction. "Quieting the mind" is one thing, but the brain is an organ like any other in the body: It has a job to do. One of the things it can do for you is anticipate threats, react to them, preserve your life, and help you predict and avoid future danger. That's a good thing.

Instead of fighting your brain's attempts to keep you safe, try to *redirect* that energy and give your mind something else to chew on.

The Bottom Line:

Our mindset as we ask and answer this question for ourselves will determine our perception of risk and our willingness to try something new.

When we focus on fearful and negative outcomes to this question, we are likely to feel out of control. To gain control we act to reduce uncertainty, which means doubling down on the status quo and potentially missing out on good opportunities.

When we focus on the possibilities we might explore and discover, however, we are more open to perceiving and responding to those possibilities. Instead of freezing in fear, *away* from threat, we allow ourselves to be guided forward, *towards* interesting possibilities. **Courage is not the absence of fear, but rather the assessment that something else is more important than fear.**

Chapter 18: Choose Hard Things for an Easier Life

The lazy and undisciplined attitude is built on a fundamental lie: Consistently taking concrete action towards your consciously chosen goals is *hard*. Being disciplined and focused means choosing a life that is *difficult*. The other side of the lie is that instant gratification is *easy* and straightforward.

But consider how the choices between easy and hard things play out over time. You could choose the easy path through your career, for example, avoiding extra responsibility, neglecting to upskill, doing the bare minimum, and consistently taking the easy route.

One day, you notice a decade or two has passed and you feel profoundly stuck. You're working for a mediocre paycheck that you are not in the position to negotiate, and alternatives seem thin on the ground. You struggle for money, for self-esteem, for personal satisfaction. You're bored, and what seemed like an easy path now feels like a prison. It's relentless, and it goes nowhere. You don't have any leverage to change your position, and you can't see a way out. Your life of easy choices has led to a hard life.

A truly difficult life isn't one where you sweat through early mornings, study while tired, or choose broccoli over fries. It's the one where you no longer get to make choices. It's the one where your world shrinks down to the size of your courage and ambition. Freedom, as they say, isn't free. It's earned, day by day, choice by choice. It's a mistake to consider working to build your own freedom to be "hard" while simultaneously thinking that forfeiting this work is "easy."

Getting fit and strong is hard. Learning something valuable is hard. Building something new is hard. Keeping consistent routines is hard. Maintaining healthy relationships is hard. Acquiring mastery and financial independence and living virtuously and keeping your word to yourself day after day is hard. If it's worth anything, it's hard to do.

The truth, however, is that these things are only *temporarily* hard. They're only hard while you're doing them. It's hard for the few days you must press through on an extremely difficult work challenge, but how much future easiness does that earn you in your career? Turning down junk food is hard for the few minutes you do it, but how does that compare to a future where you enjoy a healthy, strong, and pain-free body?

Life *is* hard. But we can choose what kind of hard. The alternative is a life that's hard because it's full of dead-end jobs, rotten health, poor relationships, relentless responsibilities, and inescapable consequences.

Instead of thinking solely in terms of easy and hard, remind yourself that what's really hard is to live a life without freedom. A narrow, limited life. The better your choices today, the more you get to live on your own terms tomorrow. Discipline doesn't just mean you force yourself to develop a taste for the hard life. It means you're making strategic decisions now precisely because you want an easy life later.

Hard Now, Easy Later

Change Your Filter

It's the long-term thinking again. Undisciplined people tend to look at options available in the limited present, and ask themselves, "Which choice is easier right now?"

The decision to consistently choose the easy path is misguided, but it comes initially from the frame placed around the power to choose in the first place. It's only human to want ease and comfort, and to avoid self-depletion for nothing. However, before you hit the snooze button, plonk yourself down on the sofa for a Netflix marathon, or order expensive takeout, change the frame and instead ask yourself, "Will this decision make my life easier or harder in the long-term?"

Discipline doesn't mean you make the perfect choice every time. It just means that overall, you make more "hard now" choices than "easy now" ones. It means you have a correct view of what you're actually doing when you skip that gym session you promised you'd do, and what you're actually giving up by making that choice. Discipline is never easy, but it's more probable when it's connected meaningfully to your ultimate future freedom.

Schedule Your Struggles — Don't Wing Them

When left to chance, hard things feel even harder. Be proactive, and decisively choose to do difficult things, on your own terms. Feeling as though an unfair world is making unavoidable demands on you just creates a feeling of resistance and resentment. It makes a genuinely beneficial choice feel like a punishment. But it's a privilege.

Pick your battles and be purposeful. Deliberately set aside 30 minutes to chip away at an important task, for example. Dedicate a Sunday afternoon to decluttering, batch cooking, or reading, or schedule in the admin tasks you've been avoiding. If you simply tell yourself that these things need to be done, but you're vague about when and how, then you're asking yourself to do far more than you need to. Visualize your future self enjoying more freedom and comfort because of what you're about to do.

Reframe Pain as Proof

When something is difficult or boring or unpleasant or even outright painful, what does that *mean*?

Your perspective makes all the difference.

The undisciplined mindset sees discomfort as a signal that something is wrong. It grabs hold of that as justification to stop. To do less. To avoid and retreat into comfort and indulgence.

Invert this mindset and tell yourself that discomfort is actually a sign that you're on the right path and doing precisely what you need to be doing. Think of unpleasant sensations in the present almost like receipts — you're actively trading in comfort now for capability later on. You're going to convert this momentary discomfort into lasting future value.

The Bottom Line:

When you feel bad and want to quit, remind yourself that you're not doing any of this because it's easy. You're doing it because you want an easy life.

Hard choices = easy life. Easy choices = hard life.

Chapter 19: Only Worry About What You Can Control

Discipline is the controlled outlay of effort and intention. It's about bringing your life under the control, regulation, direction, order, and authority of higher order organizing principles.

When we are disciplined, we choose to spend our given budget of time and energy in this life on the things that are the most meaningful and worthwhile to us. This doesn't just entail making the right choices and decisions. It's also a way of managing how we spend our own mental budget. Discipline is a way to consciously choose where your attention, awareness, and emotional investment goes.

Potential threats out there in the world are technically unlimited. But your ability to process them is not. It may feel like you can worry endlessly about an infinite number of things, but when we worry about those things we cannot control, we are taking away mental energy that could have been spent on things we *can* control. Mismanaging our worry in this way is 100% a question of discipline.

In the mind, anxiety and worry forms a shapeless mass. In reality, there are different kinds of worries. Broadly, there are worries about things we can control, and worries about things we can't. The former may encourage you to act to improve your situation. The latter will only deplete and upset you... which will also reduce your ability to act.

Cultivate the discipline to discern the difference between situations that you can control, and those you cannot, and *then* cultivate the discipline to consistently train your attention towards those things you can.

Consider Your Spheres of Control

Imagine three nested or concentric circles, like a bull's eye. Moving from the innermost circle outwards, we have:

- *The circle of control*
- *The circle of influence*
- *The circle of concern*

Just like a bull's eye, the full force and power of your attention should preferably be focused right in the center, on those things you can realistically change. In life, *most* things are not under our direct control. Like it or not, our sphere of control is rather small, and the bulk of what happens out there in the universe falls into that vast, outermost circle.

What *can* you control?

You can choose what to do with your body (to a large extent!) and you can choose what you say and do. You can choose what thoughts you entertain and what feelings you dwell on, your reactions, your attitudes, and where you place your attention and awareness. This is not to say that control in this realm is easy, just that it's possible.

Zooming out, there are some things that are not exactly under our control, yet there is nevertheless some possibility of influence. We can make choices that influence what *other* people do with their bodies, thoughts, feelings, reactions etc. We can persuade, communicate, ask, demand, contribute, nudge, manipulate, negotiate, or force.

The final circle, the circle of concern, is where we lack even this possibility of influence. We can't control whether the sun rises, or what has already happened in the election of a country on the other side of the world, or something that happened five hundred years ago. We cannot control accidents, spontaneous illnesses, or that most mysterious of all mysteries — other people's inner worlds.

It is a symptom of a lack of emotional and mental discipline to squander energy on that outer circle, while simultaneously neglecting to focus on the only things that you do have an impact on. Being stuck in the outer circle of concern means frittering away valuable time and energy on things like whether people like you or not, climate change, cancer, your mortality, what's in the past, and the fate of humanity in general.

It is an error to assume that just because something is important and emotionally weighty that you are also thus required to stress about it. Consider a financial metaphor. There is a world of things out there to buy, but you cannot buy all of them, because you only have a finite amount of money. The mere presence of a nice item or a good deal doesn't compel you to purchase it. In the same way, not every situation, idea, or dilemma that crosses your field of awareness deserves to be bought into, either.

A disciplined mind can be like a knife, cutting a clean line to separate out what is under our purvey, and what isn't. We cannot control that we have been born with a genetic condition. We can control our lifestyle and the support we seek. We cannot control the poor decisions of our children. We can control how we raise them, and how we respond to their free-will choices. We cannot control who becomes president. We can choose who we vote for.

Ask: "Which circle is this in?"

Is this situation one that is in my control?

Most things in life are complex and interconnected, so black and white answers to this question are uncommon. You can also ask, however, "What parts of this situation *can* I control? How?"

If it's hard to determine whether or not you have control, encourage yourself to think in terms of actions you can take. Can you realistically, reasonably, and practically do something to help the situation? If you can, then stop worrying and start acting. If you can't, then you will need discipline to let go of the issue or cultivate a little Stoic acceptance.

Start a "Control Log"

There are *always* things in life that are under your control. Focus on those. Some days you may have more control than others, but you always have options, and you always have the free will to choose your attitude.

Sometimes it's not even necessary to try to increase how much control you have over your life circumstances; instead, you can usually accomplish a lot by choosing to acknowledge and wisely use the control you already possess. Don't forfeit what possibilities you have by focusing relentlessly on the possibilities you wished you had.

Each day, write down three small things you can act on. Then train your mind to stay focused on these things. One of the best ways to quench anxiety and worry is to blot it out with intelligent, strategic action. Discipline your mind to stay precisely where your influence actually lives. You'll feel less stressed and more powerful.

Use Worry as a Trigger

Worried? Good. Your brain is trying to help, and it senses a problem that needs solving. So move that worry into something productive by taking action. Use your feeling of worry, rather than feeding that worry endlessly.

Try to think of concern as nothing more than a little notification bell bringing your attention to something *potentially* important. Instead of remaining in worry, shift into a more neutral and strategic gear. Try to determine the validity of the perceived threat, and whether it really is important. Remember that something can be important... and *still* not be within your sphere of influence.

Reassure yourself by taking a small active step in the right direction, or, if no action is possible, switch your attention to acceptance or simply ignoring that little notification bell. It can ping if it likes. But you are the one who decides whether or not to give it attention.

The Bottom Line:

Cultivate the serenity to accept what you can't change, the courage to change what you can't accept, and the wisdom to know the difference.

Don't bind yourself with the chains of desire and fear to things that are outside your sphere of control.

Chapter 20: Apply What You Learn

Reading without action is like collecting recipes and never cooking. It might look and even feel productive, but you'll never actually learn to cook this way, not to mention you won't produce anything real to eat.

In the same way, reading "life-changing" books and clever articles on behavior modification mean nothing unless you are actually *doing* something to change your life or modify your behavior.

It's an unflattering truth, but some of the world's most *stuck* people are those whose bookshelves are groaning with all the latest self-help and motivational literature. If you first believe that reading is in any way equivalent to acting, this is an easy trap to fall into. Reading is one of life's most fruitful habits, but it alone can only do so much.

Reading makes you a better reader. Reading and *applying* what you learn makes you a better person. It is seldom enough to read along, understand, experience a pleasant emotional reaction, or highlight a few moving quotes here and there. The reason why is painfully obvious: If you choose to go right back to living as you always have the moment you finish that last page, then your nonfiction reading may as well have been fiction.

We can assign part of the blame to authors, influencers, and book marketers for feeding the misconception that reading something true and affirming is in itself a kind of magical, transformative act. People read books on quantum mechanics and feel smart. They read weighty books on social issues and feel like responsible citizens. They read personal development books and feel like they are developing.

There is a subtle self-deception we fall into. We are like that person who shows up to therapy and is taken aback when the therapist challenges them to really work on their issues. "But... I'm here in therapy, aren't I?" The truth is that they had secretly hoped that they could "go to therapy" *instead of* genuinely having to do work to get better.

The trick out of this kind of self-deception is to challenge yourself to learn something, not to learn *about* something. Do not allow yourself to believe that gathering information is the same as actively living in the world. On the other hand, do not assume that merely liking or agreeing with a motivational message means that the message is valid, useful, or applicable in any way.

Reading is not the same as learning, nor is it the same as transforming. But it can be an important first step.

How to Turn Reading into Real Results

Read What Solves a Problem You're Actually Facing

A book is a tool, not a talisman. It's not a consumer product you proudly display on a shelf after reading, but something you actively *use* to solve real problems in your real life. Ignore the pressure to buy trending books from high-profile authors riding whatever marketing spiel they've designed to maximize profits.

Instead, read something because it promises to help you answer the questions you're facing in your life right now. When the timing fits, the lessons stick.

Run Experiments

When something speaks to you, don't just highlight it or think, "hm, that's interesting." You'll have forgotten it completely before the hour is over. Instead, test the principle on real people or in real situations. You're not reading about someone else's life, you're trying to see what your life looks like overlaid with these new principles, tools, and ideas.

Not only will this help you weed out hype and sweet-sounding nonsense, but it will also calcify within you all those ideas that truly do have the power to change your life.

Try just one suggestion from a book per week. Test it out and notice what happens. Expect that you may need to make fine adjustments. Reading a book is one thing, but give yourself time to digest what you've read, and let that information percolate into wisdom, so it can flow out in practical ways.

Revisit the Books That Changed You

Don't worry about book count; worry about book *impact*. If a book is especially meaty, return to it for another round. You'll likely discover there's more to glean. Rather than seeking out the next title, reread those books that have already made you think, feel, or act differently. As you evolve, so too will your perspective, which means that every time you approach that classic, it will have something new to share with you.

By the same token, don't be afraid to check in with books that you thought would resonate but didn't. What didn't click last year may suddenly make a world of sense this year. Develop long-term relationships with books and forego quick flings and one-time reads. That way, the good stuff becomes a living guide you shape your life around.

The Bottom Line:

Reading is the beginning of wisdom. But it's just the beginning. A book is not just meant to be read; it's meant to be digested, understood, and applied.

Don't try to see how many books you can get through. Try to see how many can get through to you.

Chapter 21: Don't Speed Read!

On the surface, the idea of speed reading makes logical sense: if reading is good, and reading a lot is even better, then reading as much as you possibly can as fast as you possibly can must be a really good idea. Right?

However, studies from leading universities like MIT and UC (Rayner et. al., 2016) show that when it comes to reading, speed is simply not a significant factor. In fact, the faster you read, the less you may absorb.

There are more books, articles, and posts in this world than any single human could ever possibly read. Speed reading programs were first introduced in the early 60s, and the promise was that you could learn to gobble up 1000 words a minute or more (compared to the 300 words per minute read by an average reader). The promise was certainly appealing to a population learning to yearn for ever-increasing productivity and output.

Today, the speed-reading promise has been found to be a little too good to be true. While you can certainly learn to increase your speed, the trade-off is in accuracy and deep comprehension — all those things that ultimately make reading such a rewarding activity in the first place.

When reading, the eyes naturally pause and focus on a small section of the page at a time, before moving to the next small section. Each pause is called a saccade and lasts just 25 to 30 milliseconds. When your eyes focus in this way, everything outside that section is blurred. This means that when speed reading advocates claim you can teach your eyes to take in more information via peripheral vision are, they are pointing to a biological impossibility.

Have you ever watched someone's eyes as they read? It can be fascinating. The eyes are not robotic and rhythmic, but rather the gaze stops and starts, fixating on certain sections to grasp the deeper meaning behind each word or fragment. Your eyes may even dart back and forth to earlier sections, as though your brain is carefully picking through and processing, pausing on knotty concepts to untie them before moving on. This is not a bug of reading comprehension, but a feature.

It's how your brain unpicks the web of symbols and concepts on the page and converts them to coherent cognitive structures in the brain.

We should be suspicious, then, when speed reading gurus promise to teach us how to *prevent* these stops and starts, and instead skim swiftly over any knotty concepts. No pausing = no comprehension. Incidentally, this is why apps that present texts a single word at a time (i.e. Rapid Serial Visual Presentation or RSVP) actually destroy the brain's ability to process the meaning behind those words.

So, it may be better to think of the term "speed reading" as a misnomer. Reading — if we define that as genuine comprehension of the full meaning in a text — is by its nature *un*speedy. Skimming and scanning are helpful to quickly categorize texts, search for relevant sections, or conduct a preview before depth reading.

For reading to be worth our time, it needs to be depth reading, and that will always require time. Consider that deep reading is extremely economical; you could speed read a dozen books in a few hours but forget them all, or, in much less time, you could properly read just a few chapters from a single book and truly understand what you've read.

Can we learn to read with more swiftness and efficiency? Of course. Reading is a skill like any other, and seasoned and practiced readers are able to train their attention to carefully work through challenging texts for a full, unbroken hour or even longer. Experienced and dedicated readers can make their way through astonishing volumes and fully comprehend what they're reading. That said, there are no real shortcuts or quick fixes with reading.

Instead, aim to be a better reader, not a faster one. Aim to optimize comprehension and retention, rather than using sheer speed as a yardstick for progress.

The Value of Slowing Down
Schedule Dedicated, Uninterrupted Time

Slow reading works when it's intentional. Create a space where you will be undisturbed for a period of time, by either outside distractions or your own inner worries. Carve out that space and protect it. Imagine that your brain is pausing its ordinary thought traffic to allow for a little island of serenity to open up in your conscious mind. Many of us have weird biases and hangups about what reading is and what it means; but you are not in school, and there will not be an exam at the end. Immersing yourself in the refreshing possibility of learning something new. Take your reading time seriously and enjoy it without guilt or anxiety. Remember that reading is about much, much more than information transfer. Give yourself the luxury of *enjoying* your time with your book.

Put Away Your Phone

Screens and devices split your attention. They keep your brain in a constant condition of low-level anxiety, and trap you in a shallow, reactive state — not ideal for learning. Notice how long you are able to read without disruptions, and see, without force, if you can gently extend that duration a little at a time.

Allow yourself frequent pauses or "beats" to process what you've encountered, before continuing. This is a little like taking a breath between bites of food. It takes discipline to take those tiny breaks, and discipline to keep coming back to the task at hand.

Read to Understand, Not to Finish

Don't rush. Your brain's preferred method to absorb text is to move through it piecemeal, one tiny step at a time. So allow it to do just that. Don't worry about what's coming at the end of the book, at the end of the chapter, or even at the end of this current sentence or paragraph. Just let ideas sink in fully as they appear in your field of awareness, one at a time.

While you might guess that this is a difficult and labor-intensive way to read, somehow the opposite is true; taking your time in this way seems to create the feeling of more ease, spaciousness, and time, in the same way that eating a meal in a slow and leisurely way leads to easier and simpler digestion.

As you read, allow your brain to build internal webs of meaning. Don't let your eyes just run along the page, internally sounding out the word and assuming that recognizing the word means you've comprehended the meaning.

Catapult.

Your brain can easily scan over the letters of this word. It probably took you a fraction of a second to sound out the word in your mind and conclude, "Yes, catapult. I know that word." But you haven't really *read* it until you've paused and mentally summoned the deeper concept of "catapult." Might this word have a few subtly different meanings?

As you read, dialogue with the text. Ask it questions, pose objections, and continually look for the many little links and connections to be made. Read and re-read. Treat each paragraph like a pleasant garden and, rather than sprinting through to get to the other side, take your time and meander.

The Bottom Line:

Nobody ever learned anything in a rush. Slow down, immerse yourself, and savor what you read.

Anything worth doing in life is worth doing slowly.

Chapter 22: The Pygmalion Effect

The Pygmalion effect is also called the Rosenthal effect, after the renowned psychologist who described the phenomenon. The Pygmalion effect is "the phenomenon whereby one person's expectation for another person's behavior comes to serve as a self-fulfilling prophecy."

In Greek mythology, Pygmalion, "detesting the faults beyond measure which nature has given to women," decided to sculpt from marble his perfect woman. He falls in love with her, and she eventually comes to life and marries him. Today, the myth is used as a shorthand to describe the way our own beliefs and expectations can figuratively carve out a role for the people we apply them to; whereas Pygmalion was a sculptor, we can shape people with our words, assumptions, and beliefs about them, to such an extent that that those beliefs take on a validity of their own, just like marble coming to life.

The Pygmalion effect is a feedback loop, however. Our beliefs about someone alter our attitude and behavior towards them. This influences the way that person sees themselves, and how they in turn choose to behave. Seeing this behavior reinforces our own original estimation, and fulfils our expectations. In other words, our perception of others influences their perception of themselves, which influences their behavior... which in turn re-influences our perception of them.

Interestingly, the power of this effect can go either way. If a teacher persistently has low expectations of his students, he may assign overly easy tasks, lower the bar and offer minimal support and feedback, not to mention subtly convey the inevitability of his students' failure. The students dutifully fulfil that assigned role. On the other hand, a teacher who expects the best will probably behave in ways to encourage, support, and pre-empt that excellence in his students, making it that much easier for them to respond accordingly.

We all know about the power of accountability and social pressure, but the Pygmalion effect goes a little deeper than this. Humans cannot help but see themselves through the eyes of others. No matter how much we might like to think that we don't care what others think, the truth is that other people's beliefs about us are one of our most important sources of self-knowledge. If someone believes in us, we tend to think they're right!

If somebody has greater faith in the best possible version of us, instead of the worst possible version, a little magic happens and we tend to find ourselves acting in ways to justify their assessment. We start to see ourselves through their eyes. We round ourselves up to that vision they have of us.

Be Mindful of the Expectations You Have of Yourself

Let's go deeper.

It's possible to deliberately use the Pygmalion effect on ourselves, in our own life. The first way is to consciously choose to surround yourself with people who have high expectations of you. At the very least, you'll be mildly shamed into not letting them down, but much more likely is that you will find yourself living up to their high estimation, rather than lowering that estimation down to where you think it should be.

Remember that this effect is cyclical and self-amplifies. Each tiny chip of the sculptor's chisel is a behavior. Act like a success so that others see. Encourage them to expect that same again, and more. Then watch as not only their behavior towards you changes, but your own behavior changes, too.

Make Your Goals Public

To get the self-amplifying cycle of the Pygmalion effect started, you'll need to take what's in your head and go public with it. Don't keep your ambitions and intentions a secret. Instead, make yourself and your goal visible, perhaps by texting a friend, saying out loud what you intend to do, or even recruiting the help of a more formal accountability buddy, putting your commitments down in black and white.

When you set up a potential image of your future self, you create a kind of productive tension. Your mind draws a line between where you are now, and that future self. Just by setting a goal, you've given yourself a metric against which to measure your actions in the present. Does what I'm doing bring me closer to that Self I've envisioned?

By basing your choices on this future self, and not your current self, you are in effect applying the Pygmalion effect to yourself, too. The more you can identify emotionally with that version of yourself, the more natural it will feel to behave in ways commensurate with that self.

Be Clear, and Be in a Hurry

Be specific. "Work on project" won't cut it. Say: "I'll finish the first draft by Friday at 6 p.m." The clearer and more defined the target, the stronger the follow-through. Pygmalion the sculptor didn't just passively daydream about his perfect woman; he got to work drawing that image out from hard marble, one difficult scrape and scratch at a time.

What's more, he actually finished his endeavor, which is more than many of us can say about projects we claim to really care about. Set yourself a deadline — a little tighter than is strictly comfortable — and make a run for it. If you expect that you can do a lot in a short space of time… then that's really what you'll do. If you expect that your tasks are tedious, insurmountable, and never-ending, then you'll fulfil your own expectation about that, too.

Treat your own self-belief like a powerful placebo. Expect to be surprised, anticipate success, and be ever so slightly too optimistic.

Report Back — Even If No One Asks

Tell someone when you've finished something important, and what you've accomplished. Allow everyone — yourself included — to subtly update their picture of who you are, and what you're capable of. This simple habit maintains a healthy sense of pressure and accountability, and makes your success feel earned.

Finally, don't argue with people when they praise you or correct them when they assume that you're more capable than you believe you are. See yourself through their eyes and correct your own self-appraisal.

The Bottom Line:

Expectations matter — both yours and others'. Project the image of the person you want to be into the present, and challenge yourself to catch up to it.

Nobody rises to low expectations.

Chapter 23: Stand Firm, No Matter What

Ganbaru (頑張る) is one of those words that doesn't have a precise translation in English. Japanese for "stand firm" or "do your best," this expression captures an attitude more than it does an exact set of actions. Perseverance in the face of difficult circumstances, and willingness to *stand firm* until the end — this is the spirit of resilience and dedication and can be considered an expression of discipline. It will come as a surprise to nobody that the Japanese take pride in their work ethic, and "Ganbaru!" is often uttered during tough times when encouragement is sorely needed.

What is wonderful about the word and the concept of Ganbaru is how plainly it acknowledges the fact of adversity in life. Doing your best is always admirable, but there may be a separate, additional set of skills needed to endure life's truly grueling episodes. When things get tough, stamina may dwindle, hopes may shrink, and all the usual coping mechanisms wear thin. It's at times like these that we need to know how to *push on anyway*. Not because it's easy, or because we know what we're doing, or because we're fired up with passion or conviction. We keep going just because we have to find a way to see things through.

Many of us have never had the opportunity to test just how much grit we are capable of when it counts. Most of the time we power along fueled by optimism, luck, and things going our way just often enough to keep us encouraged. But when we're faced with a seemingly immovable obstacle, a big challenge or a setback that threatens to topple us, all we have to fall back on are our own resources. We can almost think of Ganbaru as a kind of adaptive stubbornness — the sheer unwillingness to agree that the game is over, and you can give up now.

Figure Out What Holding Firm Means for You

Imagine a Samurai, bound by an unbreakable covenant to pursue his goal and never give up until it is accomplished. A noble picture of strength and single-minded conviction.

Imagine also a stubborn and misguided Japanese businessman who simply refuses to abandon a doomed business venture, losing money, time, and goodwill in the process. This is *not* a picture of strength or conviction, but of stubbornness.

What's the difference?

How can we use the Ganbaru principle intelligently, rather than mangling it to fit modern corporate hustle culture?

Pick One Thing Worth Fighting For

Focus on one meaningful goal instead of spreading your energy thin. When you stand firm, by necessity you stand in one place. You will have more conviction, and more potent conviction, if that conviction is singular. If you promise yourself that you will follow every single project to its completion, no matter what, you are simply paving the way to burnout. Instead, commit to finishing one thing at a time.

Be discerning about what you will pour your unwavering conviction into. In Japan, certain ingrained cultural attitudes have been found time and again to have dangerous outcomes *when practiced indiscriminately*. Blind obedience to authority may even cost lives, and create situations where rigid tradition is stifling honest growth and development. When practiced *indiscriminately*, ganbaru drives people to pointless exhaustion, or loyalty to a path that you should have abandoned a long time ago.

The solution is to be committed, but in a focused way. Try not to glorify dedication until it resembles stubbornness. Be flexible and open when considering what may deserve your attention, but once you've carefully decided on an area of focus, stand firm in that.

Consider finally that standing firm in your commitment to act in one area also requires standing firm in your commitment to *not* act in all other areas. It takes discipline to consistently say no to things that are simply not priorities. Be disciplined enough to stand firm despite other people's demands or expectations, and be disciplined enough to resist the demands you may place on *yourself* to give the appearance of high performance and ultra-productivity.

Show Up Daily, Even in Small Ways

Ganbaru does not mean perfection. A couple cultivates a good marriage not when their relationship is flawless or trouble-free, but when they can maintain commitment despite inevitable flaws and troubles. It's the same with our firm commitment to the things that matter to us. No two days are identical, and our actions will vary from one circumstance to the next, but our underlying commitment *doesn't* change. The way we move towards our goal may change from one moment to the next, but what never changes is that we are, always moving toward that goal.

Progress comes from showing up consistently, not perfectly. While Ganbaru seems like the stuff of mythical heroes, in reality we can stand firm in our commitments simply by refusing to give up. If we turn up every day and take small steps in the right direction, we are standing strong against the daily temptations to neglect our goals or make excuses for ourselves.

Some days will be hard. Try to institute the "no zero days" rule, and agree with yourself that no matter what, you will always do something towards the goals that matter, until those goals are accomplished. That may mean writing 500 words a day on your novel. If you're swamped at work one day and feeling unmotivated, however, that may go down to 200 or 300 words. If you're recovering in hospital after an operation, you may only manage 10 or 20 words a day. But you stand firm in your commitment.

The size of the action is less important than its consistency. Standing firm may look different day to day, but each of those days links up to a long, unbroken thread of choices you have made leading you towards your goal. The only guarantee of failure is to stop trying.

Cultivate the discipline required not to let a small slip up turn into a big one. If you've cheated on your diet and eaten an unhealthy meal, be honest about what's happened, and then draw a line. Stand firm and commit to not make a one meal mistake into a day of bingeing. If your next action is in the right direction, a small slip is all it will ever be. Have the discipline to not convert a small slip into a total failure.

Forgive the small slips and celebrate the small wins. The biggest battles are fought on these tiny, moment-by-moment battlefields. The discipline war is won by attrition — by small, consistent steps, every single day.

Rest Without Guilt

It may sound counterintuitive, but taking breaks is part of lasting perseverance. Pace yourself and budget your energy for the long-game — remind yourself that you have nothing to prove to others, and you do not need to give the appearance of valiant effort. Sometimes, getting comfortable in the quiet strength of your unwavering commitments is the most powerful thing you can do.

If you're trying to endure a very difficult season in life, be like the guard standing watch at the gate of the palace: settle in and take frequent naps if you need to... but don't abandon your post.

For some of us, the discipline of Ganbaru may mean having the courage and humility to acknowledge that if you are in it for the long run, you need regular rest. Work hard but take a day off every week. Take the long view. The break you take today may lead to less work being done today, but in the long term it allows for *more* sustained work tomorrow, and for the tomorrows after that.

The Bottom Line:

Stand firm in your commitments. Understand, too, that brittle things break before they bend; "firm" may not always look the same day to day.

Perseverance is not a long race. It is many short races run one after the other.

Chapter 24: The Five-Minute Rule

Imagine waking up one day and discovering an email sitting in your inbox. It's asking you to confirm a date for a meeting that's taking place a month from now, and to reply with a tiny piece of additional information needed for that meeting. Seems straightforward. Nevertheless, such a "small task" can derail entire days, weeks, even months of your time, and gobble up truly mind-boggling amounts of mental energy. Here's how such an insignificant task can jeopardize everything:

You think, "It's just a small thing, I'll do it later when I have time."

Then you don't have time. The next day it's still there in your inbox, looking at you. Registering its presence takes a little fragment of your attention and time and triggers a tiny stress response. You may not even realize it, but every time you become aware of this unfinished task, it releases a tiny crackle of negativity into your life. In fact, so long as that "small task" sits there unresolved, it will continue to emit low-level stress into your life.

You may put off answering this email for another day, and another, and each time you do so, the task grows in psychological size and weight. It now becomes A Thing. It starts to take on permanency and inevitability in your life. It begins to very, very subtly cast a shadow over everything else, especially if it's just one of many tiny tasks you've put off and avoided. In the end, it starts to feel bigger than it is. You really start convincing yourself that this task is quite difficult, quite loathsome, and each day that passes where you don't get rid of it once and for all is another day of "proof" of just how difficult and onerous the task is.

Long story short: It usually takes less time to do a small task than it does to *not* do it.

The five-minute rule is ultimately not even about discipline, but about making your life easier and less complicated: **If a task takes five minutes or less to do, then do it right away. End of story.**

Avoidance, delay, and procrastination make an insignificant task bigger than it ever needs to be. It's far easier to *just do it* than it is to try and find excuses not to do it. If you act at once, you don't have to remember anything, and you don't have any additional work to do, such as scheduling or planning how and when you'll do it. Most importantly, you are not burdening yourself with constant, low-grade stress. You are not carrying around the uneasy psychological weight of knowing, "I have outstanding tasks to do."

Don't Let Things Build Up

Nothing can jeopardize your discipline faster than the "mental clutter" that comes with a pile of incomplete tasks. There's a reason why grudges, unpaid debts, and unfinished business supply so much of the narrative drive in horror movies: on a deep level we all understand that things left outstanding create tension and unease until they are put right again.

Don't let things build up. Maintain consistent mental hygiene and keep your internal desktop clean — for your own sake. Of course, you need to plan tasks and be strategic in how you act. But that doesn't apply to truly small tasks, like those that will only take five minutes, such as replying to a short email. Have the discipline to not make more work for yourself by planning things out and kicking the can down the road.

Don't accumulate unnecessary items on your To Do list. The irony is that such a To Do list may give you an inaccurate sense of busyness and overwhelm, and ultimately *prevent* you from taking action — not to mention create a feeling that you are too busy to do anything else that might be meaningful. Procrastination is hard work. If you really want to let yourself off the hook, start by getting small tasks off your back as quickly as possible.

First, Tidy Up Any Backlog

Take a glance at your current To Do list. If it's full of things like "wash a few dishes," "sign document," or "put overnight bag by the front door," then you may need to do some intense decluttering. Your To Do list itself may not be a symptom of your procrastination, but a cause.

Once your list is streamlined, then begin to apply the five-minute rule every day, and with every new task that comes your way. Will this take five minutes or less? Then just do it now.

Find Your Flow

Procrastination is a complex problem. It's a question of time management, discipline, *and* mindset, i.e., your perception of the difficulty of a task, and your self-rated ability and willingness to complete it.

The five-minute rule is a way to keep small tasks small, so they don't become big tasks — either literally or psychologically. There is discipline in finding a productive flow that is nevertheless sustainable and comfortable. The five-minute rule does *not* mean that you drop everything to rush to complete any random task that demands your attention. If you're in deep work, then maintain your focus where it needs to be. An incoming task may only take five minutes to do, but that five minutes can begin after you've finished the current task. When you're in your flow, you can comfortably turn down intrusive calls, distractions, and demands until later. The key is not to carry that psychological burden.

The Five-Minute Rule for Bigger Tasks

The ability to make psychologically large things seem smaller and more manageable is precisely what makes this rule applicable to tasks that take longer than five minutes, too. The rule just needs a slight adjustment: **If a**

task feels intimidating, commit to making just five minutes of intense effort.

Mentally agree with yourself that it really is just five minutes. If after five full minutes of good-faith effort you still find the task difficult and unbearable, then you can stop. Try again later. There may be some missing pieces, or you may need additional support or guidance to complete the task well.

What usually happens, however, is that after five minutes, you will have broken your psychological inertia and drastically reduced the perceived difficulty of the task, making it feel much less intimidating. In just five minutes you will have neutralized the fear of never actually starting this task — because you would have already started it.

Just get moving. You don't have to see the whole staircase to take the first step. With each step, more of the staircase will come into view — no need to get stuck at the foot of the staircase planning. If you're unsure, go for the low-hanging fruit and do the easiest or most obvious task first. When you consciously break the procrastination cycle like this, not only do you get things done, but you simultaneously prove to yourself that you are not stuck, and you are not incapable.

The Bottom Line:

Procrastination is getting stuck under the weight of mental clutter. Clear the decks and free yourself.

Procrastination is the art of making a long job out of a short one.

Chapter 25: Understanding Consistency

"Be consistent!"

These words have appeared perhaps dozens of times in this book so far. But what does consistently actually look like, day to day?

Anyone can have a good day. Sometimes, the stars align and you hit it out of the park. You're fired up with motivation, your energy levels are high, external circumstances seem to line up in your favor and the right choice feels easy to make.

Does being consistent mean that we have to somehow find a way to make *every* day like this one?

The "no zero days" approach reminds us that there's power in just showing up, consistently, even if on some days that means doing only the barest minimum.

One way to look at the question of consistency is to see that it's really neither of these two extremes. Disciplined consistency entails a kind of regular, repeated action that is independent of how we may be feeling. It is something that stands *outside* of our changing experiences of motivation, difficulty, boredom, fatigue, excitement, doubt, and so on.

Though anyone can have a good day here and there, what ultimately gets results is what you do every day. Good actions are good, but it is your *most frequent* action that really defines the nature and quality of your life. Momentum is built and maintained; gains are banked and compound over time. How?

Rely on Systems, Not Your Own Motivation

What is habitual takes no effort.

The only way to make something habitual is to do it with enough consistency for a long enough time that it becomes automatic.

Until you attain sufficient momentum of this kind, you will always be relying on sheer force of will to get yourself moving forward. And that's hard.

A disciplined life is a long game. Unfortunately, most people burn out because they are relying on short-term inspiration to power them, instead of depending on systems and habit structures that essentially make the decision for them. But repeated, moderate effort beats inconsistent intensity every time.

Try to shift your attitude from thinking that consistency means "100% motivation, inspiration and willpower 24/7," and start to reframe it as, "Habitually conforming to a pre-existing system of action — no matter how I feel or do not feel."

A three-part approach can help to create such a system.

Use Rewards

Engineer your daily routine so that consistency feels good. It will not feel difficult to stick to a daily discipline if that discipline is genuinely enjoyable! Give yourself a little reward every time you show up to do your work. What behavior you reward, how you reward, and what you reward with are entirely up to you, but set up a system and let that system take over.

It's usually best to reward behaviors (which you always have control over) and not outcomes (which you often don't). Give yourself a tiny treat for every hour of deep work you do. Indulge in a hobby or some enjoyable quiet time at the end of the day when you've met your goals. You may even choose to gamify it further and reward yourself for ongoing streaks of unbroken effort, for example, ten full workouts completed in a row, one full week without chocolate, or one milestone completed on your language learning journey. Pause to fully internalize the reward. Celebrate. Give your brain time to register how good it feels to achieve and strengthen that association between beneficial action and emotional fulfilment. "*This* feels good. Let's do more of it."

Build In Accountability

While you certainly are responsible for your actions, you are not doomed to white-knuckle it on your own through the hard parts. A good consistency system or routine leverages the motivation of *other people* and uses accountability to them as a boost for when your own motivation is flagging.

Enlist the help and support of a close friend who is on a similar path to you, or who ideally shares the same goal. Find a mentor to report to, sign up for a public challenge and connect with the group, or simply post regular social media updates holding yourself accountable while visible to others.

Remember the Pygmalion effect: If other people expect you to show up, you're more likely to.

Track Progress Visually

Most people's goals are long term and abstract. It can be difficult to maintain enthusiasm for a task where your progress is largely imperceptible or will only manifest in the very long term. Counteract this by deliberately making your progress — no matter how small — visible to you.

The power of consistency lies in the hundreds and hundreds of tiny, incremental steps in the right direction. Each tiny step will look insignificant when viewed singly, but its value is more apparent when seen in aggregate. Paint this picture for yourself, so that no step, no matter how tiny, feels insignificant.

Keep a dated journal where you can see changes and development over time. Hang up a wall calendar where you can see the accumulation of good days building one on the other. Use creative DIY trackers to register every achievement; you can be as creative as you like, for example putting a penny in a glass jar to represent every $20 saved, or draw symbols on a whiteboard to represent areas of clutter in your home. Each time you clear a pile, erase it from the whiteboard so you can visually see more and more white space appearing as you make your home more and more tidy.

The right system will incorporate and integrate all three of these elements: rewards, accountability, and graphic representation. For example, you might publicly display a small ashtray at the front door of your office. Every time you smoke a cigarette, you leave the butt in here, so that everyone can clearly see how many you've had. A fellow accountability partner in the office, who is also trying to quit smoking, agrees to put their own ashtray in the same place, clearly marked as theirs. The two of you agree that at the end of every day, the one with the fewest cigarette butts in their ashtray is required to pay $5 to the other. This simple approach builds in public accountability, visual progress, and the possibility of a reward (plus some healthy competition). Both you and your colleague are likely to quit smoking far quicker than if you had tried to do it alone and cold turkey.

The Bottom Line:

Create a system that ensures disciplined action, instead of relying on willpower and motivation. Build rewards, accountability, and visibility into that system. What will make the right action more likely today and tomorrow? Do those things.

We are what we repeatedly do. Consistency is not an act, but a habit.

Chapter 26: Make the Right Kind of Mistakes

In Chapter 3 we explored the meaning of a mistake, and how to take the power out of inevitable slip-ups by following the two-day rule — to never skip a beneficial action two days in a row. Much like the five-minute rule, the two-day rule helps you quickly recover from setbacks and avoid turning small diversions into big ones.

In this chapter, we'll explore the kinds of mistakes and errors that go beyond slip-ups or occasional failures to follow through on a commitment. Blunders and missteps in life are inevitable — including the occasional big one — but it takes discipline to navigate through and past these mistakes, and to consciously turn them to good. Though it may sound trite, the mistake itself seldom matters as much as how we react to that mistake, how we frame it, and how we use it to move forward in transformation.

It's common these days for companies to talk about creating a "culture of learning" and cultivating an atmosphere where honest mistakes aren't punished, but embraced for the role they play in helping employees reflect, learn, and do better next time. You do not need to be part of a big corporate strategy like this in order to have your own failure strategy.

For many of us, our strategy, if it can be called that, is to simply hate and fear failure, and, when it happens, to collapse into some combination of avoidance and escape. Mistakes are seen as expensive, embarrassing, unacceptable, and something to move on from as quickly as possible.

It can be tempting to think that if we are only disciplined and hardworking enough, then somehow mistakes will not feature so heavily in our lives. Truthfully, if we hope to learn and develop, failure is more or less guaranteed. A disciplined mindset doesn't shield us from mistakes but allows us to manage those mistakes wisely and productively.

Turn Mistakes Into Progress

If you stigmatize failure, you create a blind spot for yourself. Through shame and inhibition, we can dampen our awareness of our mistakes, and stop really seeing them. If we can't see them, we lose the ability to understand what they have to teach us.

Be Open About What Went Wrong

Bring mistakes out into the open. Every mistake that you imbue with shame, silence, and regret becomes a sticking point that limits your genuine progress and learning. Keep reminding yourself that the mistake is not the problem; the stagnation and loss of self-awareness that can result from a poor perspective is the problem.

Be honest about what happened and why, but have the discipline to refrain from shame and blame. Mistakes are opportunities to learn, so pause and try to glean the lesson without resorting to self-criticism or to shirking responsibility. Adopt a neutral, problem-solving attitude and become curious about your exact missteps, so that you can start thinking of ways to redirect and put things right. Whatever you do, do not hide mistakes from yourself or brush past them like they haven't happened. Instead, metabolize them. Break them down for parts. Do not come away from your mistake without a new insight.

Review and Revise Often

Your true north should be: "What's not working and how can I avoid doing that again? What is working and how can I do more of it?"

Keep checking in and, rather than dwelling on could have and should have, keep your attention on what you can try differently right now, in the present, given what you know. This instils a habit of learning instead of repeating the same cycles over and over.

You can develop a reflective practice even without an outright failure. After you complete any project or task, take a few moments to pause and note down two things that went well, and two things that didn't. Think of what you might like to carry to your next project, given what you've become aware of.

Keep Failing Forward

This adage tells us to "make better mistakes."

If failure and error are an unavoidable part of the learning process, then at least make sure that you're not learning the same lesson twice!

The best way to do this is to really *learn* and aim to never make the same mistake twice. If you refuse to acknowledge and genuinely learn from a failure, you may find yourself repeating it until you do.

Of course, there's no use in literally aiming to make mistakes, but if you are sincerely reflecting on and adapting after your mistakes, then you *will* evolve... and naturally find yourself making mistakes on the next level up. Have the courage to see these new mistakes as proof of growth.

Make a habit of acknowledging mistakes honestly, owning the mistake, reflecting on it, learning from it and making the commitment to try again. Become so comfortable with failure that when it happens, it is wholly unsurprising and unremarkable to you.

The truth is that success is not just about what you know, and what you can do. It's also about how you conduct yourself when it comes to the things you *don't* know, and the things you *can't* yet do. Fear and shame get in the way of learning. When you reframe failures (even massive, humiliating flops) as ordinary learning opportunities, you take away their sting. You give yourself permission to consider the new idea this mistake may be inviting you to consider.

The Bottom Line:

Mistakes have the power to turn you into a better version of yourself, but only if you embrace them. Make mistakes, don't let mistakes make you.

Doing things wrong is valuable. You cannot learn anything from being perfect.

Chapter 27: How Less Can Be More

Our current understanding of productivity today is *additive*, i.e., we believe that if we want to achieve more, then we need to do more. If a situation is not productive enough, then we need to keep *adding* to it — more time, more effort, more work.

To push back against this narrative, however, doesn't mean we go to the other extreme, and assume that the way to the life of our dreams is to simply do less. Expecting great results from simply dialing down effort sounds nice, but it's a pipe dream. While on some level it may be true that "less is more," it really matters what "less" we're talking about.

Kate Northrup's bestseller *Do Less* explores the idea of, well, doing less; however, there is an important distinction here. We should all probably be doing less busy work, but more of the stuff that moves us forward. In this way, it's not about more work or less work, but about elegance, sufficiency, and a neat and intelligent alignment between the actions we take, and the results we get from those actions.

Thus, discipline may be less about forcing yourself to just relentlessly increase your inputs, but rather cultivating the strategic self-awareness needed to zoom in on only those inputs that are resulting in valuable outputs for you. In other words, it is not about doing *more* work, it's about doing *what* works.

Being purposeful and discerning about what work you do (rather than just upping the quantity) lowers stress levels and frees up time, while simultaneously making you more effective. It takes discipline to ask yourself, "What is really bringing me value here? And what can I stop doing?" It then takes discipline to follow through.

The Three-Step Less Is More Process

The process below is inspired by Northrup's method, but with a few tweaks. What's important is that you don't rely on mere assumptions about what is and isn't working in your life but carefully identify clear links between the effort you make, and the actual results you're getting. Be honest and take your time.

Map Out Your Inputs and Wins

First choose just one area of your life to focus on, for example: work, health, relationships, finance, or creativity. Take a blank sheet of paper and divide it vertically down the middle to create two big columns. In the left-hand column, list out the tasks that you regularly do in this area of your life. For example, if you're focusing on your studies and education, you may list out all the work you do in this area, like reading coursework, reading additional materials, attending lectures, attending tutorials, doing past papers, and watching explanatory YouTube videos.

When you're done, turn to the right-hand column, where you will list out all your "wins" in this area. This may feel trickier, but give credit where it's due. You may write down some successful exams and tests, some big insights gained with difficult material, completed group projects, or books you've read cover to cover.

Connect Tasks to Results

The core purpose of this method is to find links between your inputs (left-hand column) and your outputs (right-hand column). You are trying to visually see the relationship between the work you do and the results you're getting. It's important to be very honest here and ask yourself which actions are actually leading to the most progress.

You may discover some interesting and unexpected patterns. You may notice that much of what you do in the left-hand column is not actually producing much of an outcome for you in the right-hand column. You may notice that a small number of tasks are connected to all or most of the outcomes, or even that some of your outcomes are resulting from an input that you've not listed.

Granted, it may be difficult to draw neat and tidy links here, but you're not looking for a perfect map. You're trying to identify misalignment. For example, you may be surprised to learn that almost none of your results come from the prescribed coursework and lectures, and that quite a bit of your success has come from the materials you've engaged with outside of the assigned coursework.

Reduce or Eliminate the Rest

Highlight all the tasks that produced genuine results for you. Then be brave and cross out everything else on that list. You've seen for yourself that these tasks do not bear fruit. That means that if you reduce, eliminate, or delegate these tasks, you will still be in the position you are now... only with more time and less stress.

Turn your attention to those tasks that are pulling the most weight, and try to think of ways to support, extend, expand, or deepen your activity in that area. If you noticed that the YouTube videos and past papers were doing the heavy lifting in most of your recent academic successes, then commit to doing more of that, and see where that leads you.

For those tasks with minimal or uncertain impact, experiment with reducing your time commitment, and reappraising in a months' time. Sometimes, busy work can play the role of a security blanket in our lives, giving us the comforting illusion of making progress while not really moving the needle.

Overall, Northrup's exercise is simply a way to shine a light on our current effort expenditure, and whether we're getting a real return on investment. The spirit of "doing less" is not literally about doing nothing or being lazy. It's about being crystal clear on which daily actions are going to yield the most meaningful and worthwhile results. Each of us gets to decide what counts as meaningful, and how much meaning to assign to each action.

This exercise can be opened up further by asking yourself a few pointed questions:

If I don't have as much in the right-hand column as I'd like, why might that be?

What can I get rid of in the left-hand column so that I have more time to do something worthwhile?

What is the biggest waste of my time in the left-hand column, and what can I do this week to reduce or eliminate it?

A Note on "Necessary Tasks"

What about things like housework, admin, childcare, commuting, food shopping and prep, exercise, or social obligations? Be extra careful when it comes to all those tasks that eat your time but seem non-negotiable. There certainly *are* tasks in life that are unavoidable, but it's worth being clear and honest about whether we truly have to do these things, or whether we've just convinced ourselves they must be done.

Not every activity has to be wildly productive or spark joy; some tasks are done for the plain reason that they need doing and can't be delegated (like brushing your teeth!). If something is taking up a lot of your time, however, look at it with fresh eyes and ask what real results it brings to your life. This task may simply not be as necessary as you think.

The Bottom Line:

Not everything in life matters, not everything is useful, and not everything concerns you. Find those things that are truly important and focus on them. Let go of the rest.

It doesn't matter how much you do if what you're doing isn't what matters most.

Chapter 28: Learn, But Learn Quickly

The ability to rapidly understand something new is one of those unfair advantages that changes everything. The life of discipline is difficult to untangle from the life of learning and education — if you want to learn, you'll need discipline, and if you want to be a disciplined person, that's something you'll need to learn.

The faster you learn, the sooner you can begin actively applying what you learn, and the more real-world opportunities for further learning you will expose yourself to. It doesn't matter if you are learning a new business skill, a language, an instrument, or something more abstract like improved emotional regulation or communication — learning swiftly and effectively will mean you spend less time stuck in second-guessing and overthinking.

Truly, one of the most disciplined things we can learn to do is not to just absorb material with more intensity and effort, but to bring more focus and intentionality to the learning process itself. The problem is that most of us habitually default to outdated study methods that were never all that effective in the first place. There is an unconscious assumption that studying implies a certain *grind*, and that there is value in old-school methods like cramming, re-reading, or rote memorization.

Instead, the three learning techniques below are the epitome of "work smarter, not harder." The DISSS method, the Feynman Technique, and the Pareto Principle are strategic ways to do more with less.

DISSS

Originally developed by entrepreneur and productivity guru Tim Ferriss, this method is about breaking down any topic into easily manageable chunks, zooming in on the aspects that matter most, getting organized, and making your actions count. Like the three-step "less is more" approach described above, DISSS is about cutting out fluff and noise and zooming in with laser-like focus on what actually matters.

The acronym stands for: Deconstruction, Selection, Sequencing, and Stakes. Though there is never any need to rush, Ferriss does highlight the need for speed, as it were. If a thing is worth learning, then it's worth learning as rapidly and efficiently as possible, so you can maximize the amount of time you have to make use of that learning. Recall also Parkinson's Law, but apply it to learning: "Study expands to fill the time available for its completion."

Deconstruction: Break It Down

Any skill or piece of knowledge is really a collection of multiple subskills and pieces of information. Carefully breaking things down into smaller elements will not only give you a deeper insight into underlying structures, but will also reduce overwhelm.

As you take an inventory of the steps and components in the learning project ahead, consider also the way you will progress through that material. Identify potential obstacles along the way, and ways you could avoid them. Be honest about personal strengths and weaknesses, and pre-emptively identify useful external sources of help and guidance as your learning unfolds.

If you were trying to learn the piano, for example, you might spend some time upfront outlining the steps in a beginner level piano program — posture, fingering, simple scales, and so on. You might also explore available resources and identify the teachers and materials that would best fit you and your unique limitations (for example, you may know that you struggle with coordination). Essentially, you are charting a learning course for yourself specifically.

Selection: Focus on the Vital Few

Next we apply the Pareto Principle, or the "80/20 rule" which we will explore in more detail shortly. Very simply, assume that just 20% of your actions lead to 80% of your results. You may have already discovered this for yourself in completing the "less is more" exercise above.

Effort and outcome tend to be unevenly distributed in life, but you can use this fact to your advantage: Identify the crucial 20% and invest most of your focus, energy, and time on that, while de-emphasizing the rest.

With our piano example, this may mean taking a few piano lessons and trying to identify the exact activities during that hour that are most impactful. These things may not always be obvious, they may change over time, and they may be idiosyncratic to you and your learning style.

Sequencing: Flip the Script

You may find yourself, with a piano teacher who does things in a certain way simply because they've always done them that way, and that's the way they themselves were taught. Though you may be a beginner pianist, it doesn't mean that you cannot be curious about this curriculum, and experiment with it. There is a lot to be gained from doing things in a nonconventional order, especially if you are mindful of prioritizing those activities you have reason to believe are really pulling the most weight.

Flip the script, play around with ordering and see if you can uncover other, potentially faster ways to mastery. Instead of structuring the lesson with scales, drills, and then rehearsing a full piece, for example, switch things around and begin with a full piece rehearsal, saving the drills for later in the lesson.

Stakes: Raise the Bar with Accountability

As we have already seen, holding yourself accountable drastically increases your sense of commitment and follow-through, and the same is true for learning. Many of us fail to learn as fast or as efficiently as we can because truthfully, we're just going through the motions. We can fool ourselves into thinking that our busy work is achieving something, but then when the exam or recital or job interview comes, we find ourselves extremely unprepared.

Why? Because we allowed ourselves to learn in a superficial, light way. We didn't take it seriously, and we didn't make every minute of study *matter*. During an exam or recital or interview, things really matter, and then we are forced to hold our efforts up against real-world, external standards.

Holding yourself accountable during study means not waiting for crunch time, but raising the bar high and holding yourself to that standard. Accountability means giving an accounting of the way you have spent your time, attention and energy. It goes beyond asking someone or something else to be a nanny; it's about being held accountable to a higher standard. It means making what you do matter.

Set up consequences or rewards for yourself. Make a public commitment or announce your intentions. Set your targets high and raise yourself to them. For our piano example, keep yourself on track and accountable by signing up for group classes with mini recitals, competitions, and exams throughout the year. Make a commitment to take part in a mini-recital six months into the future. Remind yourself that people are counting on you, and remind yourself that when you said, "I want to learn to play the piano well," *you meant it.*

The Feynman Technique

The beautiful thing about the Feynman Technique is that by using it, it is actually impossible to delude yourself that you are learning when you aren't. This technique not only shines a bright light on illusory understanding, but it also paves a neat, direct path towards genuine and deep learning on any topic.

The method is named after Nobel Prize-winning theoretical physicist Richard Feynman, who made a career breaking down complex concepts and expressing their deepest essence in simplified ways, without jargon or circular logic.

The idea is simple: If you cannot explain a concept simply (say, to a child or a layperson with no prior knowledge on the topic), then it's likely that you actually don't understand the concept yourself. The big idea is that we often confuse genuine comprehension of a new idea with rote language about that idea, or second-hand explanations that are not really explanations at all, but descriptions or tautologies. Remove the jargon and lazy language, said Feynman, and what you will be left with is real conceptual understanding — if indeed there is any. The best way to understand the sheer power of this way of thinking is to practice it in your own life, not with simple ideas but those ideas that are currently at the edge of your comprehensive ability.

Step 1: Pick a Topic

What are you trying to learn right now? Pick a topic that you are currently engaged with, particularly if your understanding is only partial in this area. You can try this method out with anything you'd like to learn, like the purpose of the stock market, why people have different blood types, or how Wi-Fi works.

Initially, just write down everything you currently (think you) know about this topic. "I think Wi-Fi somehow sends signals through the air so that phones and other devices can connect to the internet." It may be revealing just how little you really understand something, when forced to put it down this way!

Step 2: Explain It Simply to Someone Younger

Next imagine how you would explain this concept to a 10-year-old or even a 5-year-old. This means simple, straightforward language without any specialized jargon. Watch out for complicated terms that only give the illusion of explanation. If I tell a 5-year-old that Wi-Fi is a "wireless network protocol," I have not really explained anything, I have just replaced one term with another.

Instead, break the idea right down and express it without a shred of jargon or technical language. For instance, for explaining Wi-Fi you can say, "It's like invisible walkie-talkies between your phone and the internet box." Naturally, this can go quite deep, and not all of us can be theoretical physicists stripping away reality to the particle layer. The idea is not uncovering absolute truth, but identifying gaps in our own understanding, and challenging ourselves to strengthen and clarify our language.

Step 3: Fill the Gaps

If you feel stuck or uncertain, that's a good thing. It's a signal to go deeper and clarify. When you go back to your studies, you now have a clearer idea of the actual gap in your understanding, and you won't be distracted by linguistic fluff or jargon. Study again and come back to your simplified explanation.

The better your understanding, the more comfortable and confident you will be in conveying that message to others. The goal is not to convey it to them, of course. Teaching others is simply a proxy for our own self-teaching. By externalizing your own mental conceptions, you can see exactly what is needed to bring them up to scratch.

Perhaps you take a closer look at your simplified metaphors and language and realize that the description of "invisible walkie-talkies" reveals a circularity: If Wi-Fi works like a walkie-talkie, then how does a walkie-talkie work? The gap here is perhaps your own complete understanding of radio waves, and exactly how that oscillating current is transmitted and received through the air. Seeing the gaps in your own explanation helps you identify the precise areas in which you need to dig a little deeper.

Step 4: Review and Repeat

Keep cycling through this process, building more awareness and understanding. See where you are, create an initial explanation, teach it to someone else, identify gaps, try to fill them, then attempt to teach again. When you have a clear and simple explanation that holds up to scrutiny, then you can confidently say, "I understand this." You've gone beyond memorization or simply learning to shuffle the terms and labels describing a phenomenon; you have learned something real about the phenomenon itself.

The Pareto Principle

The Pareto Principle is simple: 80% of results tend to come from 20% of efforts. Now, this is not a strict mathematical truth, but rather a pattern and tendency. This means that occasionally the ratio may be 70:30 and other times 90:10. The numbers themselves aren't too important; what matters is being aware of the fact that when it comes to learning actions, not everything counts the same, or produces the same impact.

Italian economist Vilfredo Pareto was the first to describe this ratio, noticing that 80% of land in Italy was owned by 20% of its population. Though initially an observation about unequal wealth distribution, today, the Pareto Principle has been applied widely to describe any disproportionate relationship, especially when it comes to productivity and outcomes.

In the context of learning, the Perto Principle reminds us that:

20% of the study material given will make up 80% of the exam paper

20% of a language's vocabulary and grammar structures make up 80% of what you really need to be conversationally fluent

20% of the foundational algebraic concepts are responsible for 80% of your overall mathematical understanding

20% of the study techniques you use are responsible for 80% of your performance

...and so on.

The Pareto Principle is merely descriptive; using it to learn means *applying* this principle and reverse-engineering your learning process around it.

Identify the High-Impact Material

Begin by asking yourself, "What's the smallest set of knowledge or skills that will get me the biggest result?" If you're learning a new language, first just focus on the most used language elements, rather than plodding through the less impactful 80% remainder. If you're learning to code, focus only on the foundation logic structures (i.e., loops, functions, conditions) and go from there. You may need a little guidance and support identifying the 20% if you're a true beginner, but this will always be time well-spent.

Prioritize Use Over Theory

Study only matters when applied. Aim to actively and consistently bring your learning out into the arena of the real-world — you'll learn faster and more reliably than if you stay too long in theory. A good idea is to spend 20% of your time on the highest yield theory, then 80% of your time applying that theory in concrete ways. For example, don't spend five hours reading about chess moves; spend an hour reading and then four hours playing real games with a variety of people.

Relentlessly Trim the Fluff

When you focus on the less important 80%, not only are you ultimately reducing the speed and efficiency of your learning, you're also making yourself far more overwhelmed than you need to be. Fluff is stressful. But for many reasons, the world is filled with fluff — noise, distractions, and information that may or may not be relevant to you in any way.

Relax and let go of the idea that you need to master everything, cover all topics, and comb through every possible piece of material in fine detail. You don't. What's more, trying to fit it all in may well undermine your ability to pay attention to the things that matter most. Be ruthless when trimming away that 80%.

This may take a little practice, and a kind of discipline that some of us are not yet familiar with. Be selective, be discerning, and be ruthless in removing anything that doesn't directly serve your goal. You *cannot* do it all. So be choosy about what you will do and choose only what counts.

The Bottom Line:

By now you may have noticed the key theme uniting all three of these learning approaches. Whether you call it focus, clarity, or precision, each method is essentially a way to identify what matters, and to amplify that while ignoring the rest. Apply all three to your learning efforts and you will save time and energy, while increasing your progress.

Focus is the art of knowing what to ignore.

Chapter 29: Success Is the Sum of Small Efforts

The classic "before and after pic" may be inspirational, but it's deceptive: it conceals the millions and millions of tiny steps that lie between the Before and the After. Incremental change is not glamorous or exciting. Sometimes, it's not even visible. When we make goals for ourselves, we may set them according to our dissatisfaction with the status quo, and our desire for the aspirational future. But really, the last step of any process is the least important.

Enter the Japanese business philosophy of Kaizen: Very simply, kai = change and zen = good. Through small, permanent changes, Kaizen was designed to help companies inch towards more productivity. This philosophy of continual refinement, however, can also be used to increase our personal performance in life.

Gradual progress may not be especially glamorous, but that's its strength. Making small, concrete tweaks day by day is accessible, manageable, and inspiring in its own way. Kaizen is itself a method of discipline; it asks us to focus on the real world, and the beneficial actions we can take; not when some fantasy future version of ourselves is fulfilled, but right here and now.

Companies like Toyota are famous for implementing a Kaizen philosophy, but the principles apply to anyone who may be feeling burnt out or lost with their work. If you put too much pressure on yourself to perform and then get overwhelmed, Kaizen can help you relax and focus on the next good step. On the other hand, if you're feeling lost and have flagging motivation, Kaizen can also help, since it will challenge you to stay on top of regular, committed action.

Practicing Kaizen is not rocket science, but it requires a mindset shift. It means understanding that small changes *are* big changes, when the element of time and consistency are factored in. Have faith that small improvements do add up, even if they seem insignificant in the moment. A compounding daily 1% change will always carry you forward more than a drastic overnight change.

How to Apply Kaizen in 3 Steps
Set a Small, Specific Goal

It doesn't matter if your goals are financial, work-related, or connected to your health, relationships, or hobbies. Select an area of your life that you would like to improve, and take the time to outline a goal, i.e., what improvement would actually look like for you. It's OK to have big, ambitious goals (it's more than OK, in fact!) but try to translate those big goals into tasks so small and unintimidating you can easily imagine yourself doing them every day, forever.

Depending on your goal, you might find success by quietly chipping away at it a little every day (for example, writing 200 words on a novel every day, no matter what) or by compounding your actions (for example, every day you make your daily run just half a minute longer than the day before).

Remove Wasteful Habits or Obstacles

Kaizen can also be used in the other direction. Every day, commit to removing a tiny bit of something that is no longer serving a purpose or adding any value.

Slicing away clutter, inefficiency, or waste is a simple but reliable way to move forward. Make space for what matters, streamline what you can, and trim away low-values tasks, busy work, or careless error.

This could be quite literal (as in a daily commitment to throw away one small piece of trash or clutter in your home) or it can be more abstract (for example streamlining a bloated morning routine, cutting away wasted hours spent on social media, or simplifying a work routine that takes longer than it strictly needs to).

Standardize and Track Progress

Kaizen helps CEOs improve procedural efficiency, and it's historically been used to streamline factory operations and trim down the margin of error in big, industrial workflows. On an individual level, the same principle can be applied to create routine and environments that support and sustain optimal habits.

Again, the idea is not to rely solely on willpower and motivation, but to create a kind of habit-momentum that makes it easier to do the right thing. Kaizen is not about being perfect or seeking some final state of flawlessness. Rather, it's about banking those small, concrete changes and making progress really stick.

How can you create an environment that is conducive to disciplined, efficient, and effective action? Standardize your actions and keep track of them. Run a tight ship with your own routines. Track what you're doing, pay attention to what's working, and keep adjusting accordingly.

A Note on Avoiding Perfectionism

Kaizen is about continuous improvement, which will always be more valuable than delayed perfection. In chapter 4 we explored how "done is better than perfect." This attitude applies to Kaizen, too. Except with Kaizen, we realize that we are never really "done." We take an action today, and by doing so we bring slight improvement. We take another action tomorrow, and nudge ourselves forward a little more. The next day, the same again. We take care of the small changes we can make here and now, and over time, the big transformations take care of themselves.

Personal development means that, over time, what we consider "good enough" is itself evolving. Do the very best you can today, within the limits you find yourself in

— that is, in its own way, perfect. Tomorrow, do the same again.

The Bottom Line:

Excellence is not a destination, but a continuous journey that never ends.

Perfection is not attainable, but if you chase perfection, you may achieve excellence.

Chapter 30: Don't Eliminate Distractions; Eliminate Your Distractibility

By now the idea of "digital detoxes" is ubiquitous, and we've all come to associate distraction with digital distraction — notifications, glowing screens, and things that ping and buzz in the night. But Nir Eyal, author of *Indistractable*, explains that distractions are more than just digital noise, they are actually "emotional escape hatches." Getting rid of devices may help in the short term, but it doesn't address the root cause, which is our tendency to try to escape unwanted or uncomfortable emotions.

As we've seen throughout this book, discipline is about the purposeful and conscious choice to focus our attention where we want it to go. But we cannot purposefully direct our attention this way when we're distracted, right? The conventional solution is to remove the distraction, but one underappreciated alternative is to work on your own ability to resist that distraction by learning to be more comfortable with uncomfortable emotions.

What makes a digital distraction so destructive is our willingness to be pulled away from our task. Long before social media and email and endless notifications, people distracted themselves from unpleasant feelings in the moment with whatever they could find in their environment. Though our modern environment is saturated with noise and distraction, the truth is that addiction, avoidance, and the desire to flee discomfort are as old as humanity.

The world is more distracting than it's ever been, so perhaps it's not unreasonable to expect that we develop new, more powerful coping skills. Eyal recommends that we forget about *unplugging* and instead focus on *plugging in* more securely to our chosen life — to all those things *we* have decided matter most to us. This takes self-awareness and, of course, discipline.

The Anatomy of Distraction – a Four-Step Process

Identify and Reframe Internal Triggers

The next time you feel distracted and pulled away from your work, pause and notice what emotional state you're in. Notice if you're feeling bored, angry, anxious, sad, lonely, resentful, tired, or confused. Distraction is activated not by some external stimulus, but by an internal motional state that makes you receptive to that stimulus. You feel emotional discomfort, you desire to escape and avoid it and find relief, and you allow your attention and awareness to flee from the task... and run straight into arms of a waiting distraction, typically a smartphone.

The way out is to *identify these emotional triggers and reframe your experience*, so as to make yourself less receptive to distraction. Distraction comes from within, and so managing your time and attention is ultimately about emotional regulation. Try to reimagine one of three things: the emotional trigger itself, the task you're doing, or even yourself and your temperament and character.

Reframe the emotional trigger, or the task: Shift your emotional energy by reframing your expectations and interpretations. If you're anxious, for example, lower the stakes and frame the task as an exploration, rather than a performance. If you're bored, frame your task as a game to find the fun. The idea is to moderate so that you don't need to escape.

Reframe your own temperament: Shift into a growth mindset, tap into your own resilience or remind yourself that you can do difficult or unpleasant things.

By finding ways to make the task easier, less intimidating, and more fun, we reduce the emotional impulse to reach for distractions. By reminding ourselves of our own disciplined intentions, we remember that a distraction means nothing unless we agree to give it our attention.

Timebox Your Day

Open-ended free time can be deadly when it comes to focus and productivity. The devil finds work for idle hands, but if every one of your tasks has a scheduled time, and every block of time in your routine is spoken for, then getting pulled off track is far less likely. When things are scheduled, distractions lose a lot of their power.

Timeboxing is a way to dedicate your time to one purpose and one purpose only. If it's on your calendar, it's a commitment. That means your brain is spoken for. Block out portions of time and literally imagine that you are now "occupied" and are for all intents and purposes unreachable by the outside the world.

Perform a Trigger Audit

Do an honest audit of your current digital and physical environments. Notice where the bulk of your emotional triggers come from. Is it a certain app or website? Is it a particularly untidy room in your house, a particularly demanding client or colleague, or a certain difficult time of day? Once you've identified the environmental triggers that are setting the stage for distraction, remove them or put them somewhere far from you.

Replace the Trigger with a Traction Plan

Give your brain something to do instead. Don't just delete distractions; replace them with something that feels purposeful. When you notice that you're triggered, redirect your attention towards a planned action that feels productive and on course. If you feel like you hit a wall and notice the impulse to escape, just pause. You don't have to force yourself through, but instead of checking social media or wasting time online, maybe take a quick break, have a cup of tea or do something else to release anxiety and come back to baseline, such as journaling, a breathing exercise, or even a light-hearted chat with a friend to change psychological gear.

It's normal to experience uncomfortable emotions, and it's normal to want to escape them. Remove the need for a distraction, however, and increase self-awareness, and that brief emotional discomfort simply becomes something insignificant to ride out. On the other side of you resisting distraction is a renewed opportunity to double down on your commitment to the things you *actually* care about. Remember this and distractions will not feel like irresistible temptations, but more like trivial disturbances with no power to displace what has real value.

The Bottom Line:

Make plans, be intentional, be specific, and act deliberately. Reconnect to what you care about. Remember that you cannot do big things if you're distracted by the little things. Choose the big things.

Don't blame distractions for disconnecting you from your path. Don't waste time arguing. Instead, re-focus on the path and strengthen your connection to it.

Conclusion

Self-discipline is not a list of things we do. It's an attitude that we take to ourselves, to our lives, and to the things we care about most deeply.

- Be consistent. Forget about willpower and get to work creating habits, routines, and systems that make the right choice inevitable.
- Choose done over perfect, but understand that making small improvements every single day is its own form of perfection.
- Don't be alarmed or discouraged by failure or slip-ups. You determine what these things mean. Claim the power to make your next move the right one, no matter where you find yourself.
- Be flexible and be honest with yourself. Let go of busy work and comforting illusions of productivity. Figure out what is most important

and effective and do that. Let go of the rest.
- Be mindful of the environment you place yourself in, and be discerning about the company you keep.
- Remember that you're mortal and have limited energy and resources. Don't waste time. Don't waste effort. Don't waste attention. You simply don't have enough of it to waste.
- Prefer simplicity over complexity, action over theory, and growth over comfort. Have firm boundaries — especially with yourself. Focus on what you can control and don't get distracted by what you can't. Quickly clear away little tasks and keep your eye on the prize.
- When you learn, cut to the chase. Find the most impactful 20% and zoom in on it. Embrace mistakes and ask them to teach you. Expect a lot from yourself and find a way to live up to your own estimation.

At the end of the day, take heart in the fact that you *do not* need to be super intelligent, talented, or lucky to succeed in life. You also do not need to have superhuman willpower, grit, or determination. All you need is to consistently maintain a disciplined mindset.

Every day is a chance to refine your life, and to refine *yourself.* Excellence is opt-in, and every day you are granted a fresh chance to make new and better choices. Take that privilege and run with it.

www.ingramcontent.com/pod-product-compliance
Lightning Source LLC
Chambersburg PA
CBHW060559080526
44585CB00013B/616